MW01173812

LOANSMART®

MORTGAGE FORECLOSURE

RECOVERY GUIDE

A Definitive Guide For Anyone Who's Lost Their Home To

Foreclosure!

by David E. Hoffman Jr.

This is a work of creative nonfiction. Some parts have been fictionalized in varying degrees, for various purposes.

Copyrights

Copyright (c) 2022 by David E. Hoffman Jr.

Trademarks

*The **LOANSMART®** brand is registered in the U.S. Patent and Trademark Office #3,470,271 and is a registered trademark exclusively of David E. Hoffman Jr. The mark is used under license from him in connection with his mortgage banking products and services business where registered, allowable or exempted by law. The **LOANSMART®** mark is used as an indicator of the source of goods, products and services of, or relating to the mortgage banking industry.*

Disclaimer

This book is not legal, financial nor accounting advice and does not warrant any reliability, nor suitability for any purpose. All information presented herein is deemed reliable but cannot be guaranteed. No guarantee is made, given nor implied. Foreclosures are complex legal actions which require the help of one or more licensed and competent professionals. This book is a 'guide only' for informational and educational purposes and intended to serve as the basis for opening dialogue between an attorney, and potentially you, the client. If you are facing foreclosure, you should seek the legal advice of a competent Attorney, a CPA, and possibly a licensed professional such as a private investigator for mortgage surplus funds recovery..

First Edition 2023.

Authorship & Book Design by David E. Hoffman Jr.

Published by Hoffman Publishing.

ISBN: 979-8-9876438-0-8

ORCID #: 0000-0001-9651-0539

TABLE OF CONTENTS

Acknowledgments

I would like to thank God for giving me breath, who some call the God of Abraham, Issac and Jacob, Allah, and the 'I AM'. There is an order to the universe. As above, so below.

To all the people who have lost their homes to foreclosure and feel hopeless; there is a path forward to rebuild. This book is dedicated to the Henry Family, the Stevenson Family, & many other families who've suffered, despite their very best efforts to honor their commitments to their mortgage lenders. In my opinion, <u>some properties were not lost</u>. Their properties WERE STOLEN! Their case studies reveal lessons to be learned and help prevent things like this from happening again, and to help protect other innocent people.

I hope the information in this book helps you & your families. I'm forever grateful to the customers who've brought me so much joy! Without customers, I have no business. Seeing your smiles, sharing the laughs and good times were my ultimate reward! In the twilight of my years will I remember you all and smile at the thoughts of you.

Thank You!

David E. Hoffman Jr.

Author, Business Owner & Student of Life

Introduction

My name is David E. Hoffman Jr. and I'm a mortgage industry professional with over 30+ years of providing mortgage & real estate services to affluent Ultra High Net Worth (UHNW) as well as low to middle income clients. I have served as a realtor, a mortgage loan officer, a counselor, a mortgage broker and banker; and in some aspects, a wealth planner. I draw upon my case files in writing this book.

It has been a fascinating journey that began with my very first purchase of a real estate property, my first home, and my first income producing property. Thru the years and up to today, it has been a constant learning process.

Every person I've encountered was a different case, a different challenge, and had it's own unique combination of variables that led them to me, to become – their trusted advisor. I've done my best to serve every client in my capacity under the fiduciary standard to help them accomplish some of their mortgage financing goals namely by:

1) becoming educated about the many facets of mortgage products in the market;

2) how to qualify for different mortgage products;

3) how to select the mortgage product that best suits the attainment of their goals;

4) how to use the mortgage information, options and resources I provide under my **LOANSMART®** brand;

5) how to efficiently and effectively negotiate a mortgage on the best possible terms;

6) how to understand and fullfill the homeowners obligations during the mortgage servicing phase;

7) how to preserve and maintain the equity & asset to pass on generational wealth to loved ones;

8) and last but not least, **how to recover from a mortgage foreclosure.**

It's best a long time since I began my journey in the mortgage industry with the very first deal I structured successfully, decades ago. A lot has changed since then. Yet, I continue my commitment to help everyone become a homeowner thru financial literacy, the mortgage qualification process, and should something go wrong - how to recover from catastrophic life events such as foreclosure. I treat every client as a personal relationship. This relationship is part of my personal philosophy of a "Customer for Life" and my **LOANSMART®** brand. A trusted advisor is someone who is there for you not just when you need a loan, but also when many other things happen along the way to your goal of building wealth thru home ownership and passing this asset to your family to be enjoyed by them for generations to come.

Although I've helped people, companies and organizations with both commercial and residential transactions; <u>this book is written for the residential mortgage homeowners and those who've lost their home to foreclosure, or facing a threat of loss due to foreclosure. There is life after foreclosure. I hope something in this book gives you insights.</u>

8

The purpose of this book product, the **LOANSMART® MORTGAGE FORECLOSURE RECOVERY GUIDE** is to <u>help residential homeowners who have lost their home</u> due to foreclosure, failure to pay delinquent taxes or other catastrophic life events, which I cover later in this book. This book is *"A Definitive Guide For Anyone Who's Lost Their Home To Foreclosure!"*.

One of the most devasting things that can happen to a homeowner is to lose their home! This can happen due to any number of sudden unforeseen life events such as:

a) illness, resulting in an inability to work;

b) an interruption in one or more incomes in the household;

c) a divorce;

d) a reduction in salary;

e) a natural or environmentally related disaster;

f) infidelity;

g) mental illness;

h) governmental instability;

'i') global, national or regional financial meltdown, such as bank runs on deposits, etc.;

j) War;

k) theft;

l) emminent domain;

m) fraud;

n) failure to pay taxes due;

o) computer related or data error;

p) forfeiture;

q) failure to pay Home Ownership Association (HOA) dues;

r) a pandemic, such as Covid-19;

s) deed theft/identity theft;

t) Attorney, or other professional negligence;

...and several other potential causes.

    In my 30+ years, I've encountered all these events and more which caused people to be at risk of losing their homes. As a mortgage professional, I would be doing the public a grave dis-service if, as a mortgage professional, I only focused my efforts and resources on the initial phase of the 30 year mortgage relationship, namely origination or getting a home loan. There are many options to turn to, if you think you're ready to apply for a home loan.

There's a whole lot that can happen AFTER the mortgage loan is approved, funded, closed and servicing begins.

The **mortgage servicing component**, or <u>phase</u> is by far the longest and most important part of the mortgage commitment rather than the mortgage payoff. During the servicing phase, the homeowner is expected to **follow the repayment schedule** (aka 'amortization table') originally agreed to during the mortgage application and negotiation phases and as evidenced by the signatures of agreement at closing. This is commonly referred to as the 'note'.

The mortgage servicer, sometimes the mortgage company, bank, insurance company, investor, or other lender, receives the 'repayment note' of their principal disbursed at closing to pay for the purchase of the property, and <u>upon repayment in full together with interest and other costs</u>; the servicer (or lender) will or should cause the 'note' to be recorded as 'satisfied'.

Although you are technically in possession of the property, and the property may be titled in your name; it is actually the lender who owns the property until the debt is repaid. The lender will usually have a 1st lien position on your property as evidenced by the 'note'.

The lender (or another lender) may also have an additional lien on your property if they advanced any funds for your benefit at the closing to help you complete your purchase transaction.

This additional loan made to you (and the promissary note that accompanies this part of the transaction) if it is after the 1st lien position mortgage note, would be a 2nd lien position mortgage and is often called a "second" in industry or common terms.

During your possession, use, and maintenance of the property; there is an intangible (invisible) asset that is created and usually grows over the course of time, subject to other factors. What is this intangible asset? This invisible asset is powerful, and is a key to generational wealth. It is called EQUITY!

Most people can't see equity. Even more people do not know how to properly value equity. Why? Because it's difficult since your potential equity in your home is not the same as the potential equity in your neighbors' homes. In my years of experience, I frequently find that EQUITY is the most unmanaged, mismanaged, neglected, abused, and misunderstood asset I've ever encountered in the normal course of the mortgage services industry.

Equity is usually made visible when it is **REALIZED**. This means that **Equity** becomes *REAL* or realized to a homeowner when they need to touch it, use it, spend it, or trade it for something else of value. Many people **never touch their equity**, and let it accumulate until they retire as sort of their nest egg. Whether you use it or not, it's there, and must be monitored and managed.

Experience Makes A Good Teacher

When I write books, or tell stories to teach, I use experiences in my life to share lessons I've learned from family, friends, clients, and my many mentors. One of these mentors told me once, in response to his question, which was, "….so what do you want to do with your life kid?".

My response, at that time (age 19), was "….why what else? I want to get rich, so I can buy all the things I want!".

Disappointed at my answer, this mentor in particular told me in an aristocratic reply, "...it's a sad state of existence to use all the wonderful gifts and opportunities we're given to only accumulate material things.".

I've had many days and nights to think about his question, <u>my answer then,</u> and reflect upon how utterly shallow and stupid I felt.

In the many years that followed, **I've since learned that the highest use of our gifts, resources, knowledge, wisdom and connections is to help people.**

This is precisely why I've switched my focus from being a 'for-profit' based operation to a 'non-profit' based operation. *No money or material things have ever <u>lifted my spirit</u> or made me feel the way that I've felt when I'm helping someone.* I remain forever, optimistic, full of enthusiasm, and steadfast in my belief that "...Everyone deserves a chance to own their own home!". Sometimes, despite our best efforts, despite our well thought out plans and intentions, THINGS CAN GO WRONG! You may have had a foreclosure. But all is not lost. In the ashes of your loss, there just may be enough seed left to rebuild, and regain momentum.

Even though you lost the home, <u>you may not have</u> **LOST THE EQUITY!**

In this book, I hope to help those who have lost their home to foreclosure. **By way of an audit of their mortgage payment account and servicing history**; *a former homeowner* <u>may be able to identify</u> and <u>prove the amount of equity that is due and payable to them.</u> If there was equity in your home at the time of your foreclosure or loss, and **we can prove it**, then the **equity** <u>may be</u> recoverable and RETURNED TO YOU!

My role is that of a 'trusted mortgage advisor'; and NOT AS AN ATTORNEY, CPA, or even as an escheats agent, surplus recovery specialist or overages 'so called expert'. While all of the aforementioned roles are honorable, and needed, as the markets deem necessary; my unique pespective begins in the 1980's and continues to this day.

<u>Sitting on the side of the closing table with my</u> <u>interests</u> **aligned with the buyers/borrowers**, I've signed my name authorizing millions of dollars to be disbursed to sellers (and their lienholders) to help payoff settlement costs and help buyers become homeowners.

Depending on what happens after the closing, and whether or not the loan was closed and sold "with recourse", or alternatively "without recourse", there can be a reasonable expectation that should a mortgage loan I have originated, closed, funded and sold, GO INTO DEFAULT, I will definitely be called before the new financial institution to make them whole for their loss. The lender, who purchased the mortgage obligation, the notes, and the servicing from me; WILL DEMAND I, OR MY COMPANY, TO APPEAR, TO ANSWER AND MAKE THE LENDER WHOLE.

Basically, if I sold them the loan WITH RECOURSE, collected my principal back, so that I can go back to the marketplace, and re-lend the capital again; then I'm fully answerable; but usually with a certain or fixed amount of time.

The financial institution and I might share the pre-agreed understanding by contract that, "….hey, you sold us the loan; it's gone bad, it's now your problem; so you go fix it!".

So, as mentioned earlier, I started out by having my interests aligned with the buyers/borrowers in helping them purchase a home. They agreed to repay the money I advanced to them. They signed the documents as proof thereof. I may have waited a few months to make sure they begin making payments. Shortly after that, I sell the mortgage obligation (the recorded deed, promissary note, servicing rights, etc) to another financial institution. The financial institution has usually done a light or moderate review of the mortgage file, with all it's documents and it's history.

The financial institution then may purchase my originated loan, if they are satisfied with my work product, and the evidence in the file. Upon purchase, they now are the institution who is in direct position to PROFIT FROM THE SPREAD between the mortgage funds advanced at closing, at the cost or interest to me (the originating lender), and what the loan will generate in profits over the term of the loan.

This profit is called the 'total amount cost of financing' and it is required on every mortgage financing transaction as a disclosure. For example, it a buyer/borrower obtains a $300,000 loan from me which closes, funds and servicing begins; it could arbitrarily collect $900,000.00 or $600,000.00 over the life of the loan with principal, plus interest payments. That extra amount is PROFIT to the bank!

These specific amounts are detailed in each borrowers amortization table. This table expresses how much of each payment, each month, and each year made by the borrowers is applied to the mortgage interest (or cost of providing funds, aka the lenders profit), and how much each month or year is applied to the reduction of the principle outstanding loan balance.

When a mortgage loan goes into default, as mentioned earlier, and it's a mortgage loan that was sold to a financial institution 'with recourse', it is sold with a guarantee, sort of.

The financial institution buying the loan DOESN'T DO THE MAJORITY OF THE WORK in finding borrowers, educating the borrowers, gathering all the documents needed, and then aligning all the other parties to a specific closing day for specific performances, based on certain representations.

In short, the mortgage brokers or bankers do the heavy lifting and hard work of originating and closing the loan; then deliver, sell or sign over part or all of the rights to the mortgage as a lender, servicer, etc. For this role, the mortgage broker/banker earns a profit.

The financial institution buying the mortgage obligation, the file and the rights now gets to collect the bulk of the profits over the term, usually 10, 15, 20 or 30 years. That's a long time for things to go wrong. Anything can happen.

Sometimes it does. Hopefully, it doesn't.

As an incentive, a mortgage broker/banker may offer their originated mortgage package for sale to financial institutions 'with recourse', or a guarantee, sort of, that the loan will perform for at least 3 years, 5 years, 10 years, or even as long as 30 years! No mortgage broker/banker normally sells originated mortgages with a 30 years recourse term. Why? That's too long of a period to be on the hook a mortgage loan should the borrower suffer a loss, and be unable to pay. If the property values go up, and there is sufficient equity in the property, AND THEN THE BORROWER LOSES THE PROPERTY, then there is a reduced risk to the lender, who has deep pockets and sufficient capital to re-invest into the foreclosued property to bring it back onto the market, and get their capital back.

Until now, I haven't mentioned mortgage loans sold by the originating mortgage broker/banker WITHOUT RECOURSE. That's because, a mortgage loan sold 'without recourse' doesn't present much liability to the originating mortgage broker/banker. It's a 'caveat emptor' or buyer beware transaction, between two qualified financial institutions.

If the borrowers' loans go into default, the broker/banker is NOT ON THE HOOK! The loss is solely born by the financial institution buying the loan!

This is quite the norm, in the mortgage industry. Originated mortgage loans are usually sold to larger financial institutions who then retain the larger rights to larger profits long term, without recourse.

Now that I've covered the basics and background on the roles of mortgage brokers/bankers and how they relate to this book. I addressed my role 'on the side of the buyers/borrowers' earlier, but now I'd like to take the other side of the table and address the interests of the financial institutions who may now have a non-performing loan on their books. They may have investors, stockholders or even government agencies THEY MUST ANSWER TO. They do no like non-performing loans? Why? Non-performing loans are code words for 'lost profits'!

Lost profits equal lost or reduced bonuses for bankers. Bankers are rewarded for profits, but penalized for losses. So how can bankers protect profits, protect their bonuses and avoid losses with a tsunami of foreclosures?

By looking for originating mortgage bankers/brokers to buy recoursed originated mortgage loans from them.

This is where branding comes into play and this is what is different about my approach. My **LOANSMART®** **Brand mortgage business** has only sold mortgage loans with FULL RECOURSE! Even if there is no contract requiring me to do so, I would STILL HONOR any lender's request to be made whole for a loss on any loan originated at any time under my trademark namely David Hoffman Jr dba " **LOANSMART®**".

This is highly unusual for my competition to do. They simply may not understand the hidden financial benefits to adopting my philosophy.

Financial institutions can appreciate and understand the added value that if a **LOANSMART®** branded mortgage goes bad, I'll buy it back if I originated it and make the lender whole.

To be able to do this, I MUST NOW SIT ACROSS THE TABLE AS THE FORECLOSING AGENT! This now means that my interests, and the lender's interest are both aligned! This is difficult to do. If it was easy, more people would be doing this. What I mean specifically is this. It is difficult, or challenging to switch from previously representing the buyers/borrowers, and then later, in the case of a default, represent the lenders' interests in non-performing loans. I said difficult. I did not say impossible.

However, it becomes easier, or should I say, less challenging, with a re-statement of the facts. The borrowers promised to payback the principal with interest at a certain rate, on a certain schedule on a property they purchased at a certain price. If there's a default, and they've lost the home; I must now step in and either pay the lender in full, or in the alternative, pay them back within a certain amount of days.

The property that was purchased, now has a market value. Presumably, the market value will be greater than the amount now owed on the principal and interest. Hence, **there**

will be equity. <u>As per the law, neither the lender, nor the originating mortgage banker/broker now foreclosing agent (in my case, guarantor) have any legal right to retain the equity.</u>

Thus, it is just a matter of me reaching out to the original borrowers <u>not as a lender,</u> but AS THE PERSON WHO PUT THEM INTO THE PROPERTY IN THE FIRST PLACE!

I've found over the years, they're more likely to respond favorably to me, than any lawyer, or other third party attempting to resolve the default. We usually can quickly meet to re-trace what happened or went wrong from OUR ORIGINAL PLANS with respect to their goals.

It's far more economical to KEEP A CLIENT, then to pour tons of money into finding new clients and proving value to them. This is called the 'Golden Rule' standard, meaning you treat others how you would want to be treated.

Sometimes, there's a way to save the home with a bankruptcy, and utilizing the skills of a competent attorney with a blameless record and high reviews. Other times, if the original qualifying income can no longer be relied on, it's best to sell the property thru the skills of a qualified real estate brokerage firm at the HIGHEST MARKET VALUE possible.

Still, there could be a marital split or divorce and an attorney would be needed to work out the differences as to who might be entitled to profits from a sale or to retain ownership rights in a property.

In the case of a <u>foreclosed property</u>, my goal is to make the BANK WHOLE FIRST, then make sure that the buyer/borrower receives the equity that was accummulated.

Next, I seek to ensure that recovered equity funds are utilitized and leveraged to help the borrowers locate and find a replacement home or another investment property that is more affordable or better suited for their needs while taking into account the factors that caused the original foreclosure, but this time with better planning. **EVERYBODY WINS!**

I've presented what is unique about my experience and my perspective. I've been on both sides of the table; with interests aligned not only with the homeowners, but also with the banks. I know where everyone is best situated in the case of a foreclosure and that is the center of the problem, where the solution is to be found. I can clearly see each side of the problem from their viewpoint.

Summary of Introduction

As mentioned earlier, this book is not meant to be deemed as legal or financial advice. Each person's situation is different and has a number of factors all varying in degree and unknown to me at this time of writing. No client relationship is implied, exists nor is established by purchase of this book.

It is merely a guide based on the years of my experience as both a mortgage lender & a broker who unfortunately had to foreclose on borrowers' homes who failed to make the payments as agreed.

Usually, they stopped responding to my outreach efforts to help them save their homes. No bank wants a borrowers home. The bank, as well as I, only wanted the payments, because we calculated that we would make a profit, IF THEY MAKE THEIR PAYMENTS!

Speaking for myself, when forced to sell a property thru foreclosure to recover the principal that was lent; this solves any temporary lender loss; but this also causes harm to the borrower, which could have been avoided.

Now that the worst as happened; **it is possible to recover.** The funds (or more appropriately named the "EQUITY") a lender, tax collector, or other entity has left over rightfully belongs to the former homeowner.

This book, the **LOANSMART® MORTGAGE FORECLOSURE RECOVERY GUIDE** provides some insights to help you as a former homeowner recover your mortgage foreclosure equity surplus funds.

There is no guarantee that something bad won't happen in life. They can, and do, happen to anyone. What you have control over IS HOW YOU REACT TO THE THINGS THAT HAPPEN TO YOU AND YOUR FAMILY!

You may have lost the home due to foreclosure or some other event. However, just because you lost possession of your home; does NOT MEAN YOU FORFEITED YOUR RIGHT TO THE EQUITY!

Let me repeat this another way. You may have lost the house, but you may still OWN THE EQUITY and have legal rights to it. It's yours, and you have a right to claim it, BUT YOU MUST PROVE IT!

Use this guide to educate yourself & get back on track. If you are ready, pay the price of the toll, by committing yourself to learning! Each member of my **LOANSMART**® network is considered family in that we all have shared experiences relating to homeownership, learning about these experiences, sharing these experiences, and helping others. If you're ready, let's dive into this subject deeper starting with chapter 1, next.

You are about to *Learn How To Recover Mortgage Surplus Equity Funds From Foreclosure!*

CHAPTER 1

UNDERSTANDING FORCELOSURE SALES AND SURPLUS EQUITY FUNDS

Definition of a Foreclosure Sale and How It Works

Foreclosure is the legal process of a lender repossessing a property when the borrower has defaulted on their mortgage payments. A foreclosure can happen when a borrower falls behind on their payments and cannot catch up or when the borrower stops making payments altogether.

The foreclosure process typically starts when the borrower misses a mortgage payment. The lender will then send a notice of default, giving the borrower time to catch up on their payments. If the borrower cannot do so, the lender may initiate foreclosure.

The exact process for foreclosure varies from state to state. Still, it generally involves the lender filing a lawsuit against the borrower and obtaining a court order to foreclose on the property. The property gets sold at a public auction, with the proceeds going to pay off the borrower's outstanding mortgage debt. Any surplus funds from the property sale get returned to the borrower, depending on state law.

Definition of Surplus Equity Funds and Why They May Be Available

Surplus mortgage equity funds get created when the sale of a foreclosed property generates more money than is needed to pay off the borrower's outstanding mortgage debt.

For example, if a borrower owes $100,000 on their mortgage and the property is sold at a public auction for $150,000, the lender would use the $100,000 to pay off the outstanding mortgage debt, and the remaining $50,000 would be surplus mortgage equity funds. These funds get returned to the borrower, depending on state law.

Suppose the property gets sold, and more than the money obtained from the buyer is needed to satisfy the outstanding mortgage balance due to the lender, plus foreclosure costs. In that case, this may result in a deficiency with a negative balance from the foreclosure sale, and this negative balance is a mortgage deficiency.

It's important to note that foreclosure can have severe consequences for the borrower, including damage to their credit score and the loss of their home. It's always best to avoid foreclosure by staying current on mortgage payments and working with the lender to find a solution if financial difficulties arise.

When a borrower defaults on their mortgage, the lender may begin the process of foreclosure. The exact procedure for foreclosure varies from state to state, but there are generally four stages:

1. Notice of Default: This is the first stage of the fo eclosure process. The lender sends a notice to the bo rowers informing them that they are in default on their mo tgage payments and have a certain amount of time (t pically 30-90 days) to catch up on their payments.

If the borrower cannot do so, the lender may proceed with the next stage of foreclosure.

2. Notice of Sale: If the borrower cannot catch up on their pa ments, the lender will file a lawsuit against the borrower an obtain a court order to foreclose on the property. The le der ill then issue a Notice of Sale, a public an ouncement of the ate and time the lender will sell the pr perty at a public uction. The 'Notice of Sale' is advertised in a local ewspaper and placed at the property too.

3. Public Auction: The property gets sold at a public au tion, which is open to the public and often held at the co nty courthouse. The winning bidder at the auction be omes the property's new owner, subject to the outstanding mo tgage debt. The proceeds from the sale pay off the bo rower's outstanding mortgage debt.

4. Eviction: If the borrower is still living in the foreclosed pr perty, the new owner has the right to evict them. Depending

on state law, the borrower will typically have a certain amount of time to vacate the property.

It's important to note that borrowers can defend themselves against foreclosure in court. However, they must prove that they have a valid defense, such as the lender improperly calculating the mortgage payments or not following the proper foreclosure procedures.

Suppose the sale of the foreclosed property generates more money than is needed to pay off the borrower's outstanding mortgage debt. In that case, the surplus funds are returned to the borrower if they can be located, depending on state law. These surplus equity funds are sometimes called "excess proceeds" or "overages."

The foreclosure process can be lengthy, costly, and embarrassing, and it can have severe consequences for the borrower, including damage to their credit score and the loss of their home. It's always best to avoid foreclosure by staying current on mortgage payments and working with the lender to find a solution if financial difficulties arise.

Chapter 1 Summary:

It's important for you to become familiar with the process. With a better understanding of foreclosure sales and the how the equity is generated, you will be able to have more intelligent conversations with others who may be able to help you like a lawyer, a counselor, a CPA, a private investigator or even a clerk at the court house. People who may have been too busy to help previously; often will change course and help if they see you've taken steps to learn about the process or you're trying to learn.

The reason they change posture is that most people want to help; they just feel that there's so much to learn. You may be starting so far from the back of the line; that it would be too much time and effort for them to get you up to speed to help make a difference.

If nothing else, there is always something you can do.

YOU CAN LEARN!

CHAPTER 2

UNDERSTANDING YOUR RIGHTS IN THE FORECLOSURE PROCESS

As a homeowner, it's essential to understand your rights during the foreclosure process. Foreclosure is a legal process in which a lender attempts to recover the balance of a loan from a borrower who has defaulted on their mortgage payments.

The process can be confusing and stressful, but knowing your rights and taking the appropriate steps can help you protect yourself and recover surplus equity funds.

<u>Your Rights as a Homeowner During the Foreclosure Process</u>
One of the most important rights you have as a homeowner during the foreclosure process is the right of "due process" of the foreclosure proceedings.

Your lender must provide formal notice of the foreclosure, typically a "notice of default" or "notice of sale." This notice will inform you of the amount of the default and the date of the foreclosure sale.

You also have the right to dispute the foreclosure. If you believe the foreclosure is in error or the lender has not followed the proper procedures, you can file a formal dispute with the court. This legal dispute is called a "motion to contest the foreclosure."

Another right you have during the foreclosure process after the sale of the property to the highest bidder is the right to reclaim surplus mortgage equity funds. If the sale of your property results in a surplus, the extra funds get distributed to you. It's important to note that this is not a guaranteed outcome and can vary from state to state.

<u>What You Can Do to Protect Your Rights and Maximize Your Chances of Recovering Surplus Mortgage Equity Funds</u>

You can take several steps to protect your rights and maximize your chances of recovering surplus mortgage equity funds.

First, stay informed about the foreclosure process. Review the notice of default or notice of sale carefully and ensure the information is accurate. Make sure the proper procedures have been followed. You can file a formal dispute with the court if you find any errors.

Next, consider hiring an attorney. An attorney can help you navigate foreclosure and advise you on your rights and options. They can also help you file a motion to contest the foreclosure and represent you in court.

Consider communicating with the lender to see if they can agree on some terms, like a short sale, loan modification, or forbearance plan. These alternatives can be a good solution for homeowners facing a difficult financial situation.

During the foreclosure process, consider contacting a housing counselor after the 'notice of default' has been sent. A housing counselor can provide you with information about your rights and options and assist you in developing a plan to avoid foreclosure.

They also can assist you in finding the resources you need to get back on track with your mortgage payments.

Remember that the foreclosure process can vary from state to state, so it's critical to familiarize yourself with your state's specific laws and regulations.

Additionally, it is essential to note that hiring an attorney or a housing counselor will not guarantee a favorable outcome. However, understanding your rights and taking the appropriate steps can help protect yourself and recover surplus equity funds.

Chapter 2 Summary:

Although you may have faced foreclosure, you do have rights but you must take action to preserve those rights. Failure to take action, or respond to legal notices can severely impact your financial standing in recovering any funds from a mortgage foreclosure. Stay informed about the process. Consider hiring a competent attorney who specializes in foreclosures if you need help understanding the legal process and your rights.

Chapter 3

IDENTIFYING SURPLUS MORTGAGE EQUITY FUNDS AVAILABLE TO YOU

Surplus mortgage equity funds refer to the amount of money left over after a foreclosure sale when the sale proceeds exceed the mortgage's outstanding balance.

As a homeowner, it's essential to understand the process of identifying and potentially claiming any surplus mortgage equity funds that may be available to you.

This chapter will provide information on how to calculate the surplus equity funds available to you, as well as tips for accurately estimating the value of your home and determining the excess equity funds available.

How to Calculate the Amount of Surplus Equity Funds Available to You

To calculate the surplus equity funds available, you'll need to determine the difference between the proceeds from the foreclosure sale and the outstanding balance on your mortgage. The calculation is relatively simple:

Surplus Equity Funds = Proceeds from Foreclosure Sale - Outstanding Balance on Mortgage Minus The Costs of Sale

For example, if your <u>home sells for $200,000</u> in a foreclosure sale, and the <u>outstanding balance on your mortgage is $150,000</u>, *then the surplus equity funds would be $50,000.*

It's important to note that calculating the amount of surplus equity funds available is not guaranteed, and the outcome can vary depending on the state laws.

In some states, the surplus equity funds are distributed among multiple parties, such as junior lienholders or state and local governments, before any remaining funds go to the homeowner.

<u>Tips for Accurately Estimating the Value of Your Home and Determining the Amount of Surplus Equity Funds Available</u>

When determining the surplus equity funds available, it's crucial to have an accurate estimate of the value of your home.

Here are a few tips to help you accurately estimate the value of your home and determine the amount of surplus mortgage equity funds available:

1. **Get a professional appraisal**: One of the most accurate ways to determine the value of your home is to get a professional "residential appraisal." An appraiser will evaluate the condition and features of your home and the local real estate market to give you a realistic estimate of your home's value.

   Do NOT rely on third-party websites such as Zillow, Redfin, etc. These are not backed by a professional license, with a proper professional liability policy coverage, in the case of errors and omissions.

2. **Compare to similar homes in your area**: Another way to estimate your home's value is to compare it to similar homes in your area. Look at recently sold properties similar in size, age, and condition to your home. The professional real estate appraisal will give you a rough idea of your home's worth.

3. **Research the market conditions:** It is also essential to research the current market conditions of your area. Are the prices in your area rising or falling? Knowing what's happening in the local real estate market can help you understand how your home might be valued.

4. **Consider the home's features and Upgrades:** Keep in mind that elements of your home may add value, such as a pool, newly remodeled bathrooms, kitchen, and even energy-efficient upgrades. These features and upgrades can help to increase the value of your home.

5. **Be Realistic:** It's essential to be realistic when estimating the value of your home and determining the surplus equity funds available.

6. Remember that foreclosure can take a while, and the market condition may have changed.

7. Is your property in the best condition? Does it need work? If so, how much would be required to bring your parcel to the market and on par with all the other properties entering the marketplace?

8. *You MUST consider the cost of slight repairs or major rehab expenses and DEDUCT THIS COST from the most recent sales of properties within a mile of your property for your estimated valuation to be genuinely realistic.*

It's worth noting that surplus equity funds are not guaranteed, and it's essential to understand the laws and regulations of your state to be aware of what is possible to recover. Additionally, recovering surplus equity funds can be complex and time-consuming, so it's advisable to consult with a lawyer who specializes in real estate foreclosures, estate sales, asset forefeitures or an approved housing counselor for guidance.

Remember that even though you may be able to claim surplus mortgage equity funds, it does not change the fact that you will still lose your home through foreclosure if you don't cure the default.

However, understanding the amount of surplus mortgage equity funds available to you can provide some financial relief during a difficult time. **You can rebuild.**

It's also <u>worth considering</u> that, **before the foreclosure process takes place, there may be alternative solutions to avoid it**, such as: <u>loan modification,</u> <u>short sale,</u> or a <u>forbearance plan,</u> that can be negotiated with the lender and, depending on the situation, it could preserve your homeownership and allow you, the homeowners, to keep more of the equity.

When determining the amount of surplus mortgage equity funds available, it is also essential to remember that there are costs associated with the foreclosure process, such as court fees and attorney's fees. These fees get deducted from the proceeds of the sale of the home.

These costs can significantly reduce the surplus mortgage equity funds available, so it's essential to consider them when estimating the available excess equity funds.

Identifying and claiming surplus mortgage equity funds can provide some financial relief for homeowners going through the foreclosure process.

Understanding how to calculate the surplus equity funds available and accurately estimate the value of your home can help you maximize the funds you can claim.

However, it's crucial to remember that claiming surplus equity funds can be complex and time-consuming, and the outcome will vary depending on the state laws and regulations. It's advisable to consult with a lawyer or a housing counselor for guidance and consider alternative foreclosure solutions before proceeding.

Chapter 4

FILING A CLAIM FOR SURPLUS EQUITY FUNDS FROM YOUR FORECLOSURE

Surplus equity funds refer to the amount of money that is left over after a foreclosure sale, when the proceeds from the sale exceed the outstanding balance on the mortgage.

As a homeowner, it's important to understand the process of identifying and potentially claiming any surplus equity funds that may be available to you. This chapter will provide information on the requirements for filing a claim for surplus equity funds, deadlines for filing a claim, and how to submit a claim.

<u>Requirements for Filing a Claim</u>

The requirements for filing a claim for surplus equity funds will vary depending on the state in which the property is located.

Generally, you will need to provide the court with evidence of your ownership of the property, proof that the sale proceeds exceeded the outstanding balance on the mortgage, and proof of your current mailing address. This typically requires the following documents:

- A copy of the notice of sale, which is the notice that the property will be sold at a public auction.
- A copy of the deed of trust or mortgage, which is the document that secures the loan on the property.
- A copy of the foreclosure sale results, which is the document that lists the proceeds from the sale and the outstanding balance on the mortgage.
- A copy of your ID or passport
- Proof of current mailing address, such as a utility bill or bank statement

It's important to note that the court may require additional documentation depending on the state laws and specific case. Additionally, some states have specific form to fill out in order to file the claim.

Deadlines for Filing a Claim

An important factor to consider when filing a claim for surplus equity funds is the deadline for filing. The deadline for filing a claim will vary depending on the state in which the property is located, but it's typically a short window of time after the foreclosure sale.

In some states, it can be as little as 30 days, while others have a deadline of 90 days. It is important to check with the court or the state's website for the specific deadline for your state.

Failure to file within the deadline will result in a denial of the claim and the homeowner will lose the chance of recovering any surplus equity funds.

How to Submit a Claim

The process for submitting a claim for surplus equity funds will depend on the state in which the property is located. In some states, the claim can be filed with the same court that oversaw the foreclosure proceedings, while in others, it must be filed with a specific department or agency.

In general, the claim must be filed in the county where the property is located and it is usually done by mail or in-person at the clerk's office. The homeowner will need to submit the required documentation and pay the appropriate filing fee, which varies depending on the state and the specific court.

It's important to keep in mind that the process of submitting a claim can be complex and time-consuming. It is recommended to consult with a lawyer or a housing counselor for guidance and to make sure that the claim is filed correctly and on time.

Once the claim is submitted, the court will review the documentation and make a determination on the claim. If the claim is approved, the court will issue an order for the distribution of the surplus equity funds.

The homeowner will receive the funds directly from the court, unless you have hired an attorney or other third party to work on your behalf to recover your funds. It's worth noting that the process can take several months.

The **recovery of surplus mortgage equity funds is not a guarantee** and it can vary from state to state. Some states distribute the surplus funds to other parties before the homeowners, like junior lienholders or state and local governments, and in some states, there is no process of recovery for surplus equity funds. There was a recent U.S. Supreme Court case which set the standard of law, and reaffirmed that any surplus funds from a foreclosure, tax sale or other liquidation must go to the former property owner.

The amount of surplus equity funds available may be impacted by costs associated with the foreclosure process, such as court fees and attorney's fees, which will be taken out of the proceeds from the sale of the home.

Keep in mind that filing a claim for surplus equity funds does not change the fact that you will still be losing your home through the foreclosure process. Understanding the amount of surplus equity funds available to you can provide some financial relief during a difficult time.

Before proceeding to file a claim, it is advisable to consider alternative solutions to foreclosure such as loan modification, short sale, or forbearance plan, that can be negotiated with the lender and, depending on the situation, it could preserve the homeownership and allow the homeowners to keep more of the equity.

Filing a claim for surplus equity funds can provide some financial relief for homeowners going through the foreclosure process. It's important to understand the requirements for filing a claim, as well as the deadlines and how to submit the claim, will vary depending on the state laws and regulations.

It's advisable to consult with a lawyer or a housing counselor for guidance and to make sure that the claim is filed correctly and on time. Homeowners should also keep in mind that the recovery of surplus equity funds is not guaranteed and the process can be complex and time-consuming, so it's important to consider the alternatives solution before proceeding.

Another important thing to consider is the fact that even if you are able to file a claim for surplus equity funds, the amount you recover may not be significant.

The surplus equity funds are calculated based on the difference between the proceeds from the foreclosure sale and the outstanding balance on the mortgage.

If the outstanding balance is high, or if the property is sold at a loss, there may not be any surplus equity funds available to claim.

Additionally, it's important to understand that the process of claiming surplus equity funds can be highly competitive, and other parties, such as junior lienholders or state and local governments, may also be claiming a portion of the funds. So even if you are able to file a claim, there is no guarantee that you will actually receive any of the surplus equity funds.

Furthermore, In some states there are also limits on the amount of surplus equity funds that a homeowner can claim, meaning that the homeowner may not receive the entire amount of the surplus funds. It's important to be aware of these limits and any other restrictions that may apply in your state.

It's worth mentioning that, depending on the state, there may be tax implications related to the surplus equity funds received. It's important to consult with a tax professional to understand the potential tax consequences of claiming surplus equity funds.

While filing a claim for surplus equity funds can provide some financial relief for homeowners going through the foreclosure process, it's important to keep in mind that the process can be complex and the outcome is not guaranteed. It's important to understand the laws and regulations of your state, the requirements, deadlines and how to file the claim.

It's also advisable to consult with a lawyer or a housing counselor for guidance, and to keep in mind that there may be alternative solutions to foreclosure that could preserve homeownership and allow the homeowners to keep more of the equity. There are third party companies that specialize in assett recovery and nearly all work on a "contingent fee basis". It's also important to consider the possible tax implications, the amount of surplus equity funds that may be available and the competition for the funds with other parties, before proceeding to file a claim.

As of this writing, there is a U.S. Supreme Court case pending which will decide whether local jurisdictions have the legal right to keep any funds recovered from a sale. This is a very tough case for the Justices to render a decision on, in my humble opinion.

On one hand, the states, counties and cities need their tax revenue to pay the teachers, the fireman, the police departments, and a host of services as well as benefits that we all enjoy without a thought of who's paying for it all. This is where tax revenue is put to a good use, and takes care of things that we're individually, or even as a small group, unable to do. Well run governments with the tax revenue, can provide these big ticket services so that we are free to go about our everyday lives.

However, taking the equity from an elderly couple who's lost their home because they may suffer from dementia, Alzheimer's or a similar memory impaired disease and simply failed to remember is no task that any government representative wants on their hands either.

I propose using a new financial product to serve as a GAP between the homeowners and the tax authorities. I came up with a few ideas during a dinner party with a government official recently. During our heated debate, we came to some barebone conclusions, that we felt could work.

Chapter 5

ALTERNATIVE OPTIONS FOR CLAIMING SURPLUS EQUITY FUNDS

When a property is foreclosed on, any surplus equity funds remaining after the sale may be claimed by the homeowner, the lender, or other parties with a valid interest in the property.

Determining the distribution of these funds can be a complex process, and there may be several alternative options for claiming them.

One alternative option is working with the lender to negotiate a settlement. This can involve the homeowner and lender agreeing on how the surplus equity funds will be distributed, which can help avoid further legal action.

A successful negotiation will likely include the homeowner presenting a solid case for why they should be entitled to a portion of the funds and demonstrating an ability to make payments.

Another option is seeking the assistance of a mediator or arbitrator. Mediation is a process where a neutral third party helps the parties to come to a mutually agreeable solution, while arbitration is a process where a neutral third party makes a binding decision based on the evidence presented by the parties. Both of these forms of alternative dispute resolution (ADR) can be less time-consuming and expensive than going to court.

If the above options do not produce a satisfactory resolution, the homeowner can choose to file a lawsuit against the party responsible for distributing the surplus equity funds.

This option is generally considered a last resort and can be costly, time-consuming, and complex. When filing a lawsuit, the homeowner should consider the jurisdiction of the court and the type of claim being filed.

Additionally, hiring an attorney who is knowledgeable about the laws and regulations surrounding surplus equity funds is a must for a homeowner.

Overall, the best course of action will depend on the specific circumstances surrounding the case, including the amount of the surplus equity funds in question, the parties involved, and the jurisdiction in which the foreclosure occurred.

Homeowners must seek legal advice and representation when pursuing the above options to ensure they have the best possible chances of success.

There are several alternative options available for claiming surplus equity funds, such as working with the lender to negotiate a settlement, seeking the assistance of a mediator or arbitrator, and filing a lawsuit against the party responsible for distributing the funds. Each option has its advantages and disadvantages, and homeowners should carefully consider which option is best for their specific situation.

Hiring A Third Party Asset Recovery Specialist

As an alternative to hiring an attorney, consider hiring a third party to investigate the foreclosure sale to determine how much the property sold for and who the winning bidder was at the foreclosure auction.

Any competent individual with the knowledge, skills, and experience can assist you with obtaining the necessary documentation required to PROVE that you are entitled to the funds left over from your foreclosure sale.

Some states require a third-party asset recovery specialist to be licensed, and others do not. Most states allow a private investigator or an attorney to perform asset recovery services for the benefit of the rightful owners. Most states need more staffing or the time to track down former owners to return their funds to them.

They may prefer to work with attorneys or private investigators because they deem these individuals more knowledgeable.

Each asset recovery case is negotiated usually on a case-by-case basis and a "contingency fee basis," meaning there are no upfront or out-of-pocket costs to you, the property owner. I advance or front any money or payment of expenses and seek compensation once the funds have been recovered.

Naturally, to protect themselves from a loss, mainly when dealing with some people who are not the best at paying their bills and have had a foreclosure, they will usually ask the property owner to authorize the recovery check to be sent to the third party company or agent.

Upon receipt of the check from the former mortgage company, their attorney, the county, or the state's unclaimed funds division, the company will deposit the check with your "pre-authorized specific power of attorney" and then write you a review less their agreed upon fees.

I caution you about the fees. THEY ARE NEGOTIABLE, and I first learned about unclaimed funds in 1986.

An attorney friend told me how to contact our state's unclaimed funds division, also called "ESCHEATS," and to purchase a list of the names of everyone they were holding funds for. Back then, I paid 150.00 dollars for the list, and after receiving my money order and pre-paid postage, they mailed me a giant printout with thousands of names, account numbers, and other data.

This is a service that has been around for decades. It will continue, too, as long as people forget about accounts and lose their properties to foreclosure, tax sales, or other legal actions.

The states, the counties, and the foreclosing lenders holding these funds attempt to locate the rightful owners. They send a letter to their last address of record (usually the property they were foreclosed on) to inform them they have money available.

More often than not, the owners have moved on and left no forwarding address. This does the job of reuniting them with their money, especially difficult.

Fees that third-party firms or recovery specialists charge range from 10% to 50% of the funds recovered. I own a company, **LOANSMART® MORTGAGE CORPORATION**, a nonprofit specializing in helping low to middle-income individuals obtain home ownership. As a mortgage industry professional for several decades, I've learned the ins and outs of the mortgage business.

In short, I'm knowledgeable and have a profound experience in mortgage foreclosure. As mentioned earlier, I've even had to foreclose on houses that were in default. I didn't want to do this. But I had no choice. This left a lot of sorrow in my heart, but when the bank doesn't get its payments, it must foreclose and take the house back to settle the account and recover the principal lent out.

I switched my focus from profit to nonprofit because so many people are losing their homes, and the funds are just sitting there. There are billions and billions of funds JUST SITTING THERE, unclaimed, while the families suffer and, in many instances, struggle to put their lives back together again.

Because I can appreciate all parties' viewpoints since I have sat on both sides of the negotiating table, I'm qualified to help all parties be made whole and have a better chance of recovering from the foreclosure, albeit the lender or the borrowers who are the TRUE OWNERS of the equity.

There are so many surplus mortgage equity accounts and people out there who might claim those funds that there will always be more attorneys, private investigators, or third parties to help everyone get their funds returned to them.

When I help someone recover the funds from their mortgage foreclosure, I know precisely WHO TO CONTACT, what to say, and what to do to recover the funds owed.

<u>Types of Cases</u>
You can audit your account in mortgage servicing and audits just as the lender does. I ONLY WORK ON MORTGAGE FORECLOSURE RECOVERY to return the surplus mortgage equity to the borrowers, and I do not do other types of asset recovery. My focus is only on those transactions in the mortgage-related category.

<u>Fees I Charge</u>

I charge a ten percent (10%) contingency fee if the mortgage company returns the funds to the owner when I ask them to. If they do NOT RETURN the funds, and I'm forced to file a lawsuit; then my fee is thirty-three and a third percent (33 1/3%) of the amount recovered because I have higher expenses such as attorney fees, court costs, etc.

I'm very efficient, and I'm still in the mortgage business, so I know both sides and can appreciate both the borrower's and the lender's viewpoints.

There are many firms and private locators out there that may charge higher fees. That doesn't mean they are cheating you or doing something wrong; it just means they might have higher costs to perform the same services.

I've set my fees based on my overhead, costs, and efficiency. As I mentioned, I've been in the mortgage industry for decades.

As a nonprofit, my corporation cannot retain the earnings, and I cannot retain the earnings. These funds (less normal overhead) are placed into a fund and re-loaned back to low to middle-income borrowers to regain their financial footing and purchase another home!

This is my unique selling proposition concerning my brand of mortgage services. I use the funds that were obtained from people who lost their homes and return THOSE FUNDS TO THOSE BORROWERS. Then, the accumulated earnings from our 10% or 33% (if we have to sue) are re-loaned back to borrowers to help them buy another house and get back on their feet.

Why do I do this? Because borrowers who have been through foreclosure have been through the stress and come out on the other side with their equity intact, make the best borrowers and repeat customers! They've already faced the worst that can happen, and we were there with them! Always helping!

As mentioned previously, this is my **'customer for life'** strategy in that <u>we treat our customers like we would want to be treated,</u> and this is the cornerstone principle of my **LOANSMART®** brand.

Sometimes bad things happen. But these things, too, shall pass. Most people reclaim their mortgage equity with our help, and many people regain solid financial standing and rebuild their lives, going on to become homeowners once again.

Chapter 6

WORKING WITH AN ATTORNEY TO RECOVER YOUR MORTGAGE SURPLUS EQUITY FUNDS

When a property is foreclosed on, any surplus equity funds remaining after the sale may be claimed by the homeowner, the lender, or other parties with a valid interest in the property.

Determining the distribution of these funds can be a complex process, and working with an attorney is often a necessary step in recovering surplus equity funds.

How to Find & Hire A Good Attorney

The first step is to conduct thorough research when finding and hiring a competent and efficient attorney. Start by looking for attorneys specializing in foreclosure, real estate, or civil litigation.

You can ask for recommendations from friends and family or search online directories of attorneys. It's essential to read reviews and check their ratings. Also, look for attorneys from professional organizations, such as the American Bar Association.

Once you have a list of potential attorneys, you should schedule a consultation. During the consultation, you should ask the attorney about their experience and qualifications in handling cases similar to yours. It's also important to ask about their fee structure and how they plan to take your case.

Tips for Working Effectively With Your Attorney

Once you have found an attorney you are comfortable with, working effectively with them is crucial to maximizing your chances of success. One way to do this is by providing your attorney with all the relevant information and documents related to your case.

This might include the terms of your mortgage, the sale of the property, and any correspondence you have had with the lender or other parties involved in the case.

Another tip for working effectively with your attorney is to be prepared for their questions and to review the steps, strategies, and facts about the case before each meeting.

This can help you understand your case's strengths and weaknesses and make it easier for your attorney to prepare a solid argument on your behalf.

It's also important to be open and honest with your attorney. If you have any concerns or questions, it's best to address them with your attorney as soon as possible.

Communication is the key to a successful attorney-client relationship. It's also essential to trust your attorney's judgment, keep track of the case's progress, and have realistic expectations. Every case is unique and requires a different approach, and even with a strong case, there are no guarantees that you will recover your surplus equity funds.

Working with an attorney is often a necessary step in recovering surplus equity funds. Finding and hiring a skilled attorney requires thorough research, asking the right questions, and proper communication. By working effectively with your attorney and providing them with all the relevant information, you will be maximizing your chances of success in recovering your surplus equity funds.

If you are a client of mine, and I'm working on recovering the equity from your mortgage foreclosure, I will pay any legal fees due for your case because, under your contingency contract with me, there will be NO OUT-OF-POCKET COST TO YOU!

I utilize an artificial intelligence (A.I.) service by Lex Machina, which scans nearly all legal cases filed in the United States, reads the cases, studies the attorney profiles, and how the judges decide their cases.

With astonishing accuracy, it can predict the case's outcome BEFORE we even file it. You would be surprised to learn that often, it is not the big, expensive law firms that win cases all the time. Sometimes, there are small firms that quietly pack a mighty punch and not only succeed in court but win big.

Surprisingly, the A.I. can pinpoint an opposing counsel of our client who is overly confident, makes mistakes or promises things, and makes blatantly false statements. In cases like this, it's a smart strategy to build your case and BE READY FOR APPEAL.

Case Study – True Story

I remember a case that we worked on where the attorney was disbarred. I warned him, and he was overly confident.

He attacked, attacked, and attacked. But he needed to be made aware that he had traveled too far from the shoreline in his pursuit. It's a shame that 'street smarts' are not taught as a class in law school.

We were trying to recover our client's money, and the outcome was common sense. But the attorney chose to fight and kept telling his client he would win, and he would have had it much easier to return the client's property.

In The End – We Win!

Before we started that case, we knew we would be fighting on appeal, and that was where the real battle would be won. In the end, our client got their property returned.

We hope this is not the outcome in every case where I'm trying to reunite a borrower with their equity from their mortgage foreclosure, and we have to spend years and hundreds of thousands of dollars to win. But it has happened.

And we could only have won by having some brilliant and diligent attorneys with whom we work. The exceptional attorneys I call the 'golden ones' are out there if you know how to look for them.

Note: We can recommend an attorney based on their record of success, careful attention to detail, and the sincerity they've shown us in genuinely putting the best needs of their clients first! If I recommend an attorney to you, use the section below to **WRITE IN THE INFORMATION:**

My Attorney Referall is:_____

Firm Name: _____

Their phone#_____

Their Fax: _____

Their Email: _____

Their Address:_____

City:_____State:_____

Zip Code:_____

Their Premonition.ai Ranking Rating is:

Their Premonition.ai Report Summary is:

Their Public Reviews Feedback Rating is:

Chapter 7

FILING A LAWSUIT TO RECOVER YOUR MORTGAGE EQUITY FUNDS

Filing a lawsuit to recover surplus equity funds can be daunting, but it is sometimes necessary to regain funds that you believe are rightfully yours. Surplus equity funds are the excess funds that remain after a foreclosure sale has taken place. The lender or the government typically holds these funds, and the funds can be recovered through a legal process.

When and why you might need to file a lawsuit to recover surplus equity funds

You might need to file a lawsuit to recover surplus equity funds for several reasons. **One common sense is that the lender or the government has failed to return the funds to you after a foreclosure sale.** Despite your documented request for the return of your surplus mortgage equity funds, they may need to be more responsive or cooperative.

This can happen if the lender or the government needs to correct the amount of the surplus equity or if they fail to follow proper procedures for disbursing the funds. Another reason to file a lawsuit is if you believe the amount of surplus equity funds being held needs to be corrected. For example, if you think that the amount being held is higher than it should be, you can file a lawsuit to recover the excess funds.

Sometimes, the lender or the government may be unwilling to return the surplus equity funds without a legal battle. Filing a lawsuit may be the only way to recover the funds in these situations.

How to file a lawsuit and what to expect during the legal process

The process of filing a lawsuit to recover surplus mortgage equity funds can vary depending on your case's jurisdiction and specific circumstances. However, there are generally a few key steps that you will need to take to initiate the legal process.

1. **Gather the necessary documentation:** Before filing a lawsuit, you must gather all relevant documentation related to your case. This may include documents related to the foreclosure sale, such as the notice of sale and the deed of trust, as well as any correspondence with the lender or the government regarding the surplus equity funds.

2. **Please consult with a qualified attorney:** It is highly recommended to consult with an attorney before filing a lawsuit. A lawyer can help you understand your rights and the legal process and advise you on the best course of action for your specific case.

3. **File a complaint:** Once you have gathered the necessary documentation and consulted with an attorney, you must file a complaint with the court. The complaint should include a detailed explanation of your case and the relief you seek, such as the return of the surplus equity funds.

4. **Serve the defendant:** Once the complaint has been filed, the defendant(s) must be served with the complaint, usually via a process server. This ensures that the defendant is aware of the lawsuit and has an opportunity to respond.

5. **Discovery:** After the defendant has been served, the discovery process begins, where both sides may request documents, take depositions, and so on. This is a crucial stage of the lawsuit, allowing both parties to gather evidence and build their cases.

6. **Mediation:** In some cases, the court may order the parties to attend mediation to try and resolve the matter before trial.

7. **Trial:** If the case is not resolved through mediation, it will proceed to trial. The trial will involve both sides presenting their evidence and arguing their case before a judge or jury.

8. **Judgment:** After the trial, the judge or jury will issue a ruling, which will determine whether the plaintiff or the defendant will prevail.

Overall, filing a lawsuit to recover surplus mortgage equity funds can be a complex and time-consuming process. However, if you believe the funds being held are rightfully yours, it may be worth pursuing legal action to regain them.

It is important to note that the time frame of the legal process can vary depending on the jurisdiction and the specific circumstances of your case.

It is generally a long process that can take several months or even years to reach a resolution.

When filing a lawsuit, it is important to have a clear understanding of the legal process and to be prepared for the potential challenges that you may face. This includes having a strong case, with evidence to support your claims, and working with an experienced attorney who can help you navigate the legal system.

During the legal process, <u>several important deadlines must be met</u>, such as the deadline to file a complaint and the deadline to respond to a motion.

Failing to meet these deadlines can have serious consequences for your case, such as dismissing your complaint.

It is also essential to be aware that <u>filing a lawsuit can be expensive and may require you to pay a filing fee, court costs, and attorney's fees.</u> Considering the costs and benefits of filing a lawsuit is essential before taking action.

As mentioned in the previous Chapter 6; if I'm working on recovering your surplus mortgage equity funds after providing my work product (namely via a mortgage servicing audit to forensically account for all payments of principal, interest, taxes & insurance, as well as all equity unrecovered); I work on a contingency fee basis, meaning I take on the responsibility of all costs associated with recovering your mortgage equity. If I'm able to execute this objective the 'nice' way (meaning preparing & presenting a merit based claim for unclaimed mortgage equity funds to the holder, who acknowledges the claim, then processes the claim), then I will deduct only 10% of the recovered funds if you pre-authorize me to collect the check and remove the contingent fee from the funds and remit the balance to you within five business days, or when the disbursement check clears the particular escrow account.

Suppose the lender, the government agency, or another third party holding your funds refuses to comply with our request to return your funds within a reasonable amount of time. In that case, we will forward our LOANSMART Mortgage Servicing Audit work product to an attorney of your choosing, who will file a lawsuit, and our combined pre-negotiated contingency fee is 33 1/3% of the recovered amount.

In terms of the case's outcome, if you are successful in your lawsuit, the court may order the defendant to return the surplus equity funds to you or pay you damages. However, if you lose the case, you may be responsible for paying the defendant's legal fees and costs.

In conclusion, filing a lawsuit to recover mortgage surplus equity funds can be complex and time-consuming. However, if the funds being held are rightfully yours and your claim has merit, it may be worth pursuing legal action.

It is vital to gather the necessary documentation, consult with an attorney, and be prepared for the challenges of the legal process. It's also important to consider the cost-benefit of the lawsuit before making a decision.

Chapter 8

GOING TO TRIAL

Going to trial to recover surplus equity funds can be a complex and challenging process. Still, it may be necessary to regain funds you believe are rightfully yours. Surplus equity funds are the excess funds that remain after a foreclosure sale has taken place.

The lender or the government typically holds these funds and can be recovered through a legal process, including trial.

Preparing for a trial, including gathering evidence and witnesses

Preparing for trial is crucial to increase the chances of success in recovering your surplus equity funds. This includes gathering evidence and identifying potential witnesses who can support your case.

1. **Gather the necessary documentation:** Before going to trial, it is crucial to gather all relevant documentation related to your case, such as documents related to the foreclosure sale, correspondence with the lender or the government regarding the surplus equity

funds, and any other documents that may be relevant to your case.

2. **Identify potential witnesses:** Identifying witnesses who can support your case is also essential.

3. This may include individuals who know about the foreclosure sale or the disbursement of the surplus equity funds, such as the foreclosure sale administrator or the lender's representative.

4. **Prepare witness statements:** Prepare written statements from potential witnesses, outlining what they will testify to, if necessary.

5. **Hiring an expert witness:** In some cases, it may be necessary to hire an expert witness to provide testimony on specific issues related to your case, such as the calculation of the surplus equity funds.

6. This might include a private investigator who has been hired to prepare a report on claims when multiple heirs or the previous property owners entitled to the surplus mortgage recovery funds are now divorced.

7. When the original owners are deceased, private investigators' reports can be beneficial in shedding light for the Judge to consider where there are multiple heirs to a deceased estate.

8. **Work with your attorney:** Your attorney can help you to gather evidence and prepare your case for trial.

9. They will also be able to advise you on the best course of action for your specific case and help you to understand the legal process.

The Trial Process And What To Expect In Court

A) Jury selection vs. Judge's Decided Cases: The first step in the trial process differs depending on if the case will be decided by a Judge (A Hearing) or a trial with jury selection, where a panel of potential jurors is selected to hear the case. The attorneys from both sides will question the potential jurors to determine their qualifications and suitability to serve on the jury.

NEARLY ALL THE CASES I'VE BEEN INVOLVED WITH WERE SETTLED BY A HEARING, WITH ONLY THE JUDGE DECIDING THE OUTCOME.

B) *Rarely does the borrower have to appear for the hearing. The attorney I retain always appears on your behalf.*

C) If filing suit is required to recover your surplus mortgage equity funds, there will be a hearing, and anyone who opposes the return of your funds to you has a chance to challenge your request.

D) They may also claim they are owed part or all of your funds. However, if they do not submit an objection or a claim to any of your funds, the Judge will most likely grant the attorney's motion for your funds to be returned.

E) This is considered a simple case. In a complex case, where there is significant recoverable equity or multiple parties assert claims against the funds you have requested be returned to you, there may be a trial with either a judge or a jury.

F) Opening statements: The attorneys will make opening statements outlining their case and the evidence they will present.

G) Presentation of evidence: Both sides will present their evidence, including witness testimony, documents, and expert testimony.

H) Cross-examination: The opposing attorney will have the opportunity to cross-examine the witnesses and challenge the evidence presented.

I) Closing arguments: After the presentation of evidence, the attorneys will make their closing arguments, summarizing their case and the evidence presented.

J) Deliberation: After the closing arguments, the Judge or the jury will deliberate and decide on the case.

K) Verdict: The Judge or the jury will return a decision that will determine whether the plaintiff (YOU) will be granted the return of your funds or the other claimants/lienholders (if any) will prevail and receive part or all of your funds.

L) Order: The Judge will determine the appropriate amount of funds to be returned to you (minus the court costs and fees) and issue an Order to return the surplus equity funds to the plaintiff, co-claimants/lienholders, or to pay damages.

It's important to note that going to trial can be stressful and time-consuming, and you'll not be guaranteed to win the case.

However, if you have a strong case and have prepared well, your chances of success will be greater. It's also important to remember that even if you win the case, the defendant may appeal the decision, which could prolong the legal process.

Going to trial to recover surplus equity funds can be a complex and challenging process. It may be necessary to regain funds that you believe are rightfully yours.

Preparing for a trial, including gathering evidence and identifying potential witnesses, is crucial to increase the chances of success. During the trial process, it is essential to be prepared for the challenges of the legal process, such as cross-examination, and to work closely with your attorney to present your case in the most effective way possible.

Be aware that going to trial can be a lengthy and costly process, and it's not guaranteed that you will win the case. Therefore, it's crucial to weigh the costs and benefits of going to trial before deciding.

It's essential to have realistic expectations about the trial's outcome and to be prepared for the possibility of an appeal if the defendant is not satisfied with the result.

In addition to the above, it's also essential to be prepared to present your case clearly and persuasively. This includes clearly explaining your argument and the evidence that supports it and effectively responding to any questions or objections that the opposing attorney or the Judge may raise.

It's essential to be professional and respectful when in court, as the Judge and jury will be paying attention to your behavior and argument. This includes being punctual, dressed professionally, and maintaining a respectful demeanor throughout the trial.

Going to trial to recover surplus equity funds is a serious step and should not be taken lightly. Preparing well, working with an experienced attorney, and approaching the trial process with realistic expectations will increase your chances of success. And most importantly, always be professional and respectful throughout the process.

Chapter 9

MANAGING YOUR FINANCES

DURING THE PROCESS

The mortgage surplus recovery process can be difficult and stressful for homeowners. Not only are you dealing with losing your home, but you may also need financial help. A solid budget and financial plan during this time are crucial to help you navigate the process and minimize the economic impact on your life.

Developing a Budget and Financial Plan During the Surplus Equity Funds Recovery Process

The first step in managing your finances during the mortgage foreclosure surplus funds recovery process is to develop a budget and financial plan. A budget and financial plan will help you understand your current financial situation and identify any areas where you may need to cut back to make ends meet.

When developing your budget, it is essential to consider your income and expenses, including your mortgage payments, utilities, and other bills. You will also want to consider any additional expenses you may incur due to the foreclosure process, such as legal fees or moving costs.

Once you've got a clear understanding of your income and expenses, you can start to adjust your budget as needed. For example, if you are spending more than you are earning, you may need to make some cuts to reduce your expenses. Spending could include cutting back on luxury items or services or saving money on bills and expenses.

It's essential to consider your long-term financial goals during this process. For example, if you plan to purchase a new home, you will need to factor in the cost of a down payment and closing costs. You'll need to save money to rebuild your credit score and improve your chances of being approved for a new mortgage.

Seeking Assistance with Bills and Expenses if Necessary

If you struggle to make ends meet during the mortgage foreclosure surplus funds recovery process, several options are available to help you manage your bills and expenses.

One option is to seek assistance from government programs such as food assistance, energy assistance, and other programs that can help you with your bills and expenses.

Another option is to seek assistance from non-profit organizations and charities. These organizations can provide financial aid, counseling, and other services to help you manage your bills and expenses during this difficult time.

Speaking with creditors and service providers is essential if you struggle to pay your bills and expenses. They can work with you to create a payment plan or provide other assistance.

Exploring Options for Credit Repair and Rebuilding Credit After a Foreclosure

The mortgage foreclosure surplus funds recovery process can significantly impact your credit score, making it more difficult for you to get approved for new credit or loans in the future. However, there are steps you can take to repair your credit and improve your chances of being approved for new credit or loans.

One option is to work with a credit counseling agency. These agencies can provide counseling and education on how to repair your credit and a budget and financial plan to help you get back on track.

Another option is to work with a credit repair company. These companies can help you dispute any errors on your credit report and work with you to remove any negative information from your credit report.

In addition to credit repair, it's essential to rebuild your credit score by carefully considering new creditors you can begin and maintain a positive payment history or payment schedules you can afford. Credit can be rebuilt by making timely payments, reducing debt, and using credit responsibly.

It is also essential to monitor your credit report regularly to ensure there are no errors and that all credit applications are authorized and submitted by you. It's no secret in the mortgage industry that as a member of the mortgage industry, you must maintain an 'arms-length' transaction' when applying for a home loan yourself if you choose to do so. In the past, I was in the market to purchase a foreclosure.

A property I had identified as a potential foreclosure a year or two earlier was finally finalized. It would only finish in under two years, and I had plenty of time to sell or trade other assets and convert them to cash. I fully intended to pay cash for the foreclosure to complete the acquisition.

Then I had planned to rehab the property and either bring it back to the market and cash out on a 'fix & flip' or place a home equity line of credit on the property based on the new ARV (after repair value) and use the HELOC to return favorable positions in other projects.

It didn't quite work out that way. Anyone working in the mortgage industry has to go thru the SAME processes that any other potential homeowner goes thru, and the qualifications are the same. And most likely, an underwriter will place anyone in the mortgage industry under greater scrutiny precisely because they are IN THE BUSINESS and may know ways to circumvent checks and balances.

In my case, I needed $350,000 FAST to close on a property. There was a lot of interest in the property, so I spent my time visiting local banks and credit unions to shop for rates and negotiate a deal on the best terms I could get.

I was shocked when a loan officer I met told me there was NO WAY I would ever close on the loan because my ratios were off. It wasn't that I didn't make enough money or that my credit needed to improve. There were multiple businesses that I was personally funding, and these loans, under the law, had to be fully disclosed. The outstanding debts and scheduled monthly payments must be factored into the proposed 'Debt To Income' or DTI calculations. When the loan officer did this, I felt the loan officer incorrectly calculated my income, first by calculating my income after asking me, "How many times each month do you get a check?". I told the loan officer I usually get two monthly checks from each business.

My loan officer calculated each income source as a bi-monthly frequency when she added each income source.
In reality, I was paying myself 26 checks each year. Yet, my loan officer calculated my income on a bi-monthly basis.
There are 12 months a year, and bi-monthly payment yields 24 pay periods.

That's a vast difference and nearly knocked me out of qualifying. I went to another bank and went higher up the food chain. I own a mortgage company, so I know how the process works. The 'Corporate Level' bank officer agreed with my assessment of the miscalculation done by the other bank I applied to, BUT I was told, based on your short-term debt obligations, you need to pay those off or raise your income by about $1,000/per month. That wasn't the only challenge, which, incidentally, I knew how to solve by adding another income stream, such as starting another side hustle, getting a part-time job, selling off assets, or leasing out property for additional income.

The loan officer, who had previously told me "....that there was no way I was going to qualify," apparently was trying to make good on her prediction. She had run my credit a whopping eight times! These additional pulls of my reports WERE NOT AUTHORIZED. I did sign a written authorization to pull my credit, but I certainly did not intend for a machine gun to be sprayed on my credit report as she did.

The disgusting thing was that I didn't find this out until I went to the following bank and went HIGH UP ENOUGH to get a high-ranking bank officer who I knew could do something about it as I had done for such money others. I knew that people with specific access could request a 'rapid re-score or a manual update/correction to the borrower's credit report IF THE BORROWER HAS THE PROOF in writing.

Finding people who can do this are scarce. It can be done if you find someone who knows about this, has the experience, and has suitable credit bureau access.

With a manual update, I could get all the inquiries from the same lender consolidated into just the one query I had authorized.

I'm taking the time to bring this to your attention because there are things that can happen to your credit report along the rebuilding process IF YOU MISS THEM and you happen to get someone who isn't as knowledgeable as they think they are about all the options available to you; you might miss out on an opportunity. Other things can hamper the rebuilding of your financial profile. I wrote a book specifically on credit with more detail about this, which is part of my 'Financial Literacy Series.'

The book is the **LOANSMART®** Credit Score Guide, available on Amazon.com or Barnes & Noble. Other things can hamper your rebuilding process and hinder you when you fr obtain credit after a foreclosure.

Lenders can see applying for too many credit cards or loans at once as a red flag and can negatively impact your credit score. Instead, space out your credit applications and focus on building a solid credit history over time.

In addition, be mindful of your credit utilization ratio. A credit utilization ratio is the amount of credit you use compared to the available amount. A high credit utilization ratio can harm your credit score, so keeping your credit utilization ratio low is vital.

Finally, it would help to be mindful of your credit history. Any outstanding debts or unpaid bills can hurt your credit score. Pay all your bills on time and resolve any outstanding debts as soon as possible.

In conclusion, managing your finances during the mortgage foreclosure surplus funds recovery process can be challenging. Still, taking the necessary steps to minimize the financial impact on your life is crucial.

By developing a budget and financial plan, seeking assistance with bills and expenses, and exploring options for credit repair and rebuilding credit, you can navigate the process and get back on track financially. You can overcome this difficult time and move forward to a brighter financial future with the right approach.

It is also essential to seek professional help if necessary. Suppose you need help managing your finances during the mortgage foreclosure surplus funds recovery process. In that case, a financial advisor or credit counselor can provide the guidance and support you need to make informed decisions and achieve your financial goals.

Be aware of any laws and regulations that may apply to the surplus equity funds recovery process. In some states, homeowners may be entitled to a portion of the excess funds after selling their foreclosed home. It is essential to consult with a lawyer or other legal professional to understand your rights and any potential options for claiming these funds.

Furthermore, it is vital to consider the emotional impact of the foreclosure process. Losing your home can be a traumatic experience and can significantly affect your mental and emotional well-being. It is essential to take care of yourself during this time and seek support from friends and family, as well as professional counseling if necessary.

In summary, managing your finances during the mortgage foreclosure surplus funds recovery process requires a multi-faceted approach. It is crucial to have a solid budget and financial plan in place, seek assistance with bills and expenses, and explore options for credit repair and rebuilding credit.

Additionally, being aware of applicable laws and regulations is vital. Seek professional help if necessary, and take care of your emotional well-being. With the right approach, you can navigate foreclosure and move to a more financially stable and secure future.

Chapter 10

APPEALING AN ADVERSE FUNDS HEARING DECISION

The surplus funds hearing process can be a lot of work for homeowners. After a foreclosure sale, any excess funds left over from the sale of the property are usually held in escrow, and a hearing is held to determine the rightful owner of the funds.

If the homeowner is not satisfied with the outcome of the hearing, they may have the option to appeal the decision.

The first step in appealing an adverse surplus fund hearing decision is to understand the reason for the decision. Reviewing the hearing transcript and any relevant documents is essential to understand the reasoning behind the decision.

The hearing transcript will help you determine whether there are any grounds for appeal.

One common reason for an adverse decision is a lack of evidence presented at the hearing. If you believe that there was substantial evidence that there was not considered or that you were not an error in the interpretation of the law; or evidence you presented or were denied an opportunity to have considered, this may be a valid ground for appeal.

Another reason for an adverse decision may be an error in the legal process. For example, if the judge made a mistake in interpreting the law or the hearing wasn't conducted according to the rules and procedures, this may be grounds for appeal.

If you believe there are grounds for appeal, the next step is to file a notice of appeal with the court. This must be done within a specific timeframe, typically within 30 days of the hearing decision.

The notice of appeal must include a statement of the issues to be appealed and a request for a new hearing. There may be a cost to the court to do this, such as a court filing fee and a 'process server' fee.

After the notice of appeal is filed, the court will schedule a hearing to review the case. During the hearing, both sides will have the opportunity to present their case and argue their position.

It is important to note that an appeal is not guaranteed, and the court's decision may not favor the homeowner. Therefore, it's vital to seek the assistance of a lawyer to ensure that the appeal is adequately prepared and presented.

If the decision is still not in favor of the homeowner, they may have the option to file a further appeal to a higher court. However, it's essential to know that the process becomes more complex and expensive at this stage.

Appealing an adverse mortgage equity surplus funds hearing decision is a complex process that requires a thorough understanding of the legal process and the grounds for appeal. It is essential to seek the assistance of a lawyer to ensure that the appeal is adequately prepared and presented. While the outcome is not guaranteed, it is crucial to consider all options available to ensure that the rightful owner of the surplus funds is determined.

You may be discouraged if you've received an adverse decision against you. It's common to disagree with the court's decision, and it's also common to disagree with your attorney's course of action. Your interpretation of the law and what is right may differ from that of the attorney you've chosen.

This is precisely why you must take time and carefully consider the attorney you select to represent you. Any number of issues, factors, and circumstances could have affected the outcome of your adverse case decision. I have retained countless attorneys throughout my career, not only for myself, my companies, and my family members but also for my clients. I've found that all attorneys are different. A law firm with a good reputation in one area is only sometimes guaranteed to produce favorable outcomes with all of their attorneys and in all categories.

Some law firms specialize in certain practice areas and are usually deemed EXPERTS, and that's all they do. These law firms are recognized as the firm to go to for a specific type of legal issue that you need to resolve. This is usually reflected in the outcomes of previous cases they've handled for another client.

If they're a personal injury firm, how many of their past cases have they actually won? If they're a real estate firm, how many cases have they won for their clients as defendants or plaintiffs?

In recovering your mortgage foreclosure equity surplus, you would be well-positioned to seek an attorney with a solid and successful record of winning on appeals. Additionally, this attorney has in-depth knowledge of the real estate industry, mortgage banking, taxation, and probate. In that case, you have an excellent chance at winning the recovery of your mortgage equity surplus funds on appeal of the adverse decision.

As bleak as it may seem, don't give up. If you've chosen an attorney who lost the initial court case at the hearing and disagreed with their opinion, remember it's just THEIR OPINION. You can seek a second or even a third opinion from other attorneys.

In my experience, I value the opinions of those attorneys who specialize in the types of legal cases I'm facing more than those of attorneys who are 'general practitioners. There are many ways to lose their property besides just a mortgage foreclosure. Homeowners can lose their homes to non-payment of taxes and non-payment of Home Owners Association (HOA) dues.

Homeowners can lose their properties due to lack or failure to maintain insurance on the property at all times they borrowed against. A property can be lost due to eminent domain.

While this book addresses only mortgage foreclosure and how to recover from mortgage foreclosure, a loss of one's home is no less devasting, no matter how it, unfortunately, may happen.

COST OF APPEALING

There is a cost to appeal an adverse decision on your mortgage, which is <u>financial</u>, <u>time</u>, and <u>emotional/health-related</u>.

Financial Cost

The financial cost will no doubt involve the court filing fees (usually around $400, but they vary from state to state and at the federal district court area). In addition to the court costs (filing fees, process server fees, etc.), there will usually be a retainer fee to the attorney who researches and files the appeal. The legal costs of an appeal attorney files or generally less than the fees that are charged during the original court case.

This is because, USUALLY, there are no new issues to be raised, and the appeal will most likely be decided on things like errors in interpretation of the law, ineffective counsel, lack of due process, etc.

There are some instances where an appeal, an entirely new case with new issues, can be raised if filed that is supported by facts or facts at law. Just be very careful when choosing your legal counsel, and ensure you have a factual basis for standing before pursuing an appeal. Many legal cases have been won on appeal, and don't rule this out!

Time Cost

t will cost you not only money but your time. Is it worth your time to fight for the recovery of a few thousand dollars left over as a surplus from your mortgage foreclosure?

What is an hour of your time worth? What are you giving up if you were to direct the time you would spend on the appeal towards another project, endeavor, or to your family?

Only you know what your time is worth and what recovering what is rightly yours is worth to you. You must make this decision yourself because ultimately, YOU MUST PEACE AT PEACE WITH YOUR DECISION, no matter the outcome!

Health Cost

There is a cost to your health you must consider when deciding to appeal an adverse decision to your mortgage. You may have heard the phrase before that "Health is Wealth." This is true. What good is it to have material possessions, objects, or fame when you do not have 'good health'?

"Never do or participate in anything that will rob or diminish you of your health if you can help it.
And if you must, let it be for a short time, followed by a dedicated time to repair, nourish, and rejuvenate yourself." -
David E. Hoffman Jr.

American philosopher Ralph Waldo Emerson in 1860, wrote, "Health is Wealth. Wealth is Health". Harvard economist David E. Bloom cited Emerson in his article, reminding us that good health is a foundation for building a happy life, a community, and an economy.

I would surmise they mean that the phrase "Health is Wealth" means you have everything when you have good health. You can earn and buy whatever you want if you have good health. Being financially wealthy cannot guarantee good health, and no money can guarantee you can buy back health once it is lost or carelessly squandered.

I understand that you have suffered a loss due to your mortgage foreclosure. Anybody can replace their money. But do not lose your health, chasing money or that which is lost.

What is lost financially can be replaced. Your good health cannot quickly be recovered once it is squandered.

Looking at the chapters ahead, in chapter 11, we cover common mistakes to avoid. In Chapter 12, I will cover ways to recover from the loss financially and rebuild. Even if you are unsuccessful in your appeal, you can take the information I present in Chapter 12 and start rebuilding your life and financial foundation.

Fighting to recover your mortgage equity surplus funds will be stressful. You should hire an attorney to research, prepare and draft the appeal (and deal with the stress) than do it yourself.

Stress kills. There is no guarantee that the recovery efforts of your mortgage surplus equity funds will be successful. The focus, the anxiety, and the anguish of fighting an adverse court decision on recovering your funds can elevate your blood pressure, increase your heart rate, and severely impact your health.

Please consider the cost to your health when you are evaluating whether or not to file an appeal if the court decides at your hearing adversely against you that you are not entitled to any funds that may be left over from your foreclosure after your mortgage(s) have been paid off from the forced sale of the property.

In the next chapter 11, we'll go over some common mistakes to avoid as you recover from your mortgage foreclosure.

Chapter 11

COMMON MISTAKES TO AVOID

There are some key mistakes to avoid or key concepts aka best practices that you should adopt or practice. The list below is not by any means 'all inclusive' but it is a good start. I've included a couple of blank pages at the end of this book titled "NOTES" at the top of the page. This is perfect for you to jot down any new information you come across on your educational journey.

Here are some of the top mistakes you should avoid or conversely, the best practises you should adopt as follows:

1)   Failing to realize that you must always be learning! No one knows everything, including you and I. You must rom here on, always be on the look out for quality, verified, igh value information. The information I present in this ook, under my LOANSMART® brand is high value. Why? ainly because it is based on real life, true experience. A yone can enter the mortgage industry tomorrow and start p acticing. They may even mistakenly think that for a time, b cause they make a lot of money, they are smart, are even S ARTER than you or I. Calling oneself smart, does nto m ke them smart. Smart people , do SMART THINGS! That's exactly WHY

THEY'RE SMART. SO how do you get smart? Committt yourself to learning. Always be learning! And, never think that you are the smartest person and that you no longer need to learn. This is mistake number one!

2) **In all the things you must pay in life, ALWAYS PAY ATTENTION!** Failing to pay attention is one of the top mistakes you can make. Most likely, failing to pay attention to those letters that the mortgage company was sending prior to the default caused the foreclosure. They got no responses. Their letters were ignored. No one paid attention. The result? Foreclosure! They know exactly how to solve the problem of a b rrower who has defaulted on their promises to repay the f nds and refuses to respond.

They foreclose! They take the propoerty. They sell it at auction. They apply the funds they receive against the outstanding mortgage balance(s). Whatever is leftover, as mentioned in previous chapters, is mortgage equity surplus funds. IF THERE IS ANYTHING LEFT after all the expenses associated with the foreclosure have been paid, then these SURPLUS EQUITY FUNDS BELONG TO YOU!

3) Listening to what THEY SAY, rather than doing your own research and getting the facts! Exactly, WHO THE F*CK IS THEY? Where do they live? What do they do for a living? And what do THEY have to do with your mortgage, your forclosure and how can they help you get your funds back? Most people who give their opinions (advice) for a living, have professional liability, or at the least errors and omissions insurance to protect them, IF WHAT THEY SAY IS INCORRECT!

Opinions are the cheapest things in the world because they are usually free. Laywers have a professional license and liability insurance. They are aware that they can be sued if they give bad advice, or give poor performance that results in harm or financial loss to their clients. That's why I prefer hiring an attorney to help me recover a client's funds when they have suffered from a foreclosure and there are mortgage equity surplus funds.

If you have lost your real estate property, you will need to PROVE THAT YOU OWNED IT AND THAT THERE WERE FUNDS LEFT OVER FROM THE FORCLOSURE SALE BEFORE YOU HAVE ANY CHANCE OF GETTING ANY FUNDS RETURNED TO YOU!

4) Failing to take notes and documenting your case and recovery efforts in detail. This is self explanatory. If you do not already have a file on your former property and your mortgage account history; then you will need to re-construct your file beginning from the first day you purchased the property and continuing up to the day the file is closed, namely, when you get your equity funds returned to you.

For most people who have lost their homes, this is an overwhelming task. Fortunately, I'm one of the mortgage professionals in the United States that have the experience, the resources, connections and are committed to helping people who have lost everything get back on their feet.

5) Failing to have their mortgage servicing account audited. As you are aware, and as I have mentioned previously and in ome of my videos, mortgage servicing is a critical if not the ost important part of the home ownership process. Why? Because it is the process and accounting of CORRECTLY applying your promised mortgage repayments to your recorded debt instrument against your property.

By auditing your mortgage servicing account, you will quickly learn IF your payments have been correctly applied. You will also learn if they (the mortgage servicers) have made a mistake. It's critical for you to detect any accounting or bookkeeping errors and dispute them to have them corrected if they have made a mistake. By failing to correct any errors, and notifying the mortgage servicer of the errors and giving them a deadline to correct them, you might be inadvertently AGREEING TO THE ERRORS which might result in foreclosure.

In addition, there are certain situations where a mortgage servicer can LEGALLY RECEIVE YOUR MORTGAGE PAYMENTS AND YET FAIL TO CREDIT YOU FOR YOUR PAYMENT AND STILL FORECLOSE AND TAKE YOUR HOUSE!

Wait! WHAT?

That's right. There may be a clause in your mortgage agreement where you agreed that the mortgage service via the lender is NOT OBLIGATED T ACCEPT PARTIAL PAYMENTS!

This actually happened to one of my clients, who was a very, very intelligent person. As a result of being intelligent, this client was always busy, and always presented with opportunities to make money, always on the go. Unfortunately, failing to pay attention, this otherwise smart person, had somehow intheir minds remembered their mortgage payment to be $1,800 per month, due the 1st of each month, and NOT THE $1,813 per month as the mortgage note stated at the closing. So what happened?

So, this borrower for over two years, made payments of $1800 which the lender was not obligated to accept, but they did, and placed the funds in A SUSPENSE ACCOUNT! I repeat, they accepted the payments, but did NOT CREDIT THEIR MORTGAGE ACCOUNT and mark it as paid; they placed the funds they received into a SUSPENSE ACCOUNT BECAUSE IT WAS $13 LESS THAN THE MONTHLY AGREED TO AMOUNT!

About 2 years later, the client got a notice of default citing, you guessed it, the 24 months of $13/month payments that were obviously short. Since they were now in default, the entire amount borrowered with interest was now accelerated and due. All this could have been avoided in any number of ways. This brings me to my next mistake or errors that people make and you must avoid.

6) Failing to Open Mail or Respond to Mail and Legal Notices In A Timely Fashion. Just because you don't respond to a letter, or a notice, does not mean that you are not at risk of losing your SH!T! A mortgage lender, or servicer only has to prove they gave you notice prior to taking action.

7) Failing to Realize It is YOUR JOB To Monitor and Manage Your Investments. Even though you may have a spouse, a wife, a friend, a family member, or even a stock broker, an investment advisor, a financial advisor, or a smart friend; IT'S STILL <u>YOUR JOB</u> TO BE AWARE OF WHAT <u>YOU HAVE</u>, IT'S <u>VALUE</u>, IT'S PEFORMANCE AND HOW IT FITS INTO YOUR LONG TERM PLAN TO <u>ACHIEVE YOUR GOALS</u>!

It's ok to hear people out. Be open minded. Brainstorming with like minded individuals can produce new and better ideas, as well as opportunities. Yet, these ideas also require thought! Do your own thinking.

One curious thing that I've noticed in looking at thousands of people's credit reports, financial portfolios, and anlyzing them is this. Poor people do poor people things. Rich people, do rich people things. As I mentioned in a previous chapter real wealth is health. To me, health as a sister. This sister is TIME! Most wealthy people I know are more in control of their time, than those who are poor. I'll say it again, THEY (THE WEALTHY) OWN THEIR TIME! They simply DO WHAT THEY WANT WITH THEIR TIME! Usually!

The poor people I know, rarely, if ever, own their time. They actually value their own time very lowly, or do not know how to manage their time.

A billionaire friend of mine once told me, when I asked him how he felt about NOT WORKING EVERYDAY – he quickly corrected me and said, *"...Dave, you got it wrong, I work hard every day!"*. I laughed, but I had to say, "....well it looks like you aren't working to me. It looks like you're laying here on the beach to me, and we're catching some sun, drinking a few beers and chilling out, while everybody else is working hard busting their butts at work.".

Again, he said, *"....Dave, we are in fact working."*.

Not one to argue, I said, ".....well if this is working, then this is the type of work I'd rather be doing than doing grunt work or low value, low paying stuff.".

My friend replied, "...well then you've made a choice! You've made a choice to do with your time what YOU VALUE MOST! So why are you here Dave?".

I was confused at first, but then answered, "...I guess I'm here at the beach with you because I've reached am impasse at my office and I can't figure out how to reduce the time my employees are wasting with clients we make on low revenue generating clients. I need them to spend more time with the higher revenue generating clients! If I can do that, I'll make more money, waste less, and have more resources to do more of what needs to be done, and not only help more people, but live a better quality of life for myself. I figured being around you you, I might get some new ideads on how to solve this, or a fresh perspective.".

I'll never forget what happened next. My billionaire friend, then looked over at me, lowered his sunglasses just slightly enough so he could make DIRECT EYE CONTACT WITH ME, then he starred for about 10 seconds and looked into my eyes and said ".....*that sounds a lot like work to me Dave!*".

Then all of a sudden it hit me! He was working. Who knows what he was planning in his mind, or what problems he was addressing. I had just then realized I was working too! They didn't need me back at my office. They needed me to come back with a solution to our problem. However or wherever I came up with that solution was of no concern to them. By making the workflow more efficient, more profitable, and less monotomous; they would be happier.

I realized then that RICH PEOPLE THINK DIFFERENTLY THAN POOR PEOPLE! Just one spark, just one break thru idea can make all the difference in your life.

Just in case you're thinking right now, "...well I've gotta find me some rich people to hang out with.", you'd be wrong!

You don't need to hang out with rich people to learn from them or profit from them. You can just do what I mentioned earlier, and **PAY ATTENTION!**

Ray Dalio is well known for being smart, and his hedge fund is where rich people take their money to do what, you ask? They take their money to Ray Dalio's hedge fund to MAKE MORE MONEY! And I took notice.

So, when Ray Dalio made a huge investment for put options that basically bet the stock market would crash oh, around March 2020, I was not shocked when the Corona Virus aka Covid-19 hit the news and everything was getting shut down. Those options Mr. Dalio bought for $1.5 Billion became worth substantially more after the market crashed as a result of the Covid-19 pandemic.

Was any poor or less fortunate person thinking "Stock Put Options! Pandemic! Time to Invest!"? I doubt it. But many of Ray Dalio's clients got richer because they had their money with his fund. Like I said, **rich people, <u>think</u> like rich people.** Poor people, <u>think</u> like poor people.

IT IS A CRITICAL MISTAKE FOR YOU TO NOT OPEN YOUR MIND AND CONSIDER WHAT I'M SHARING WITH YOU IN THIS BOOK!

I understand that you may have suffered a tremendous loss. You may have lost your home. You may have lost your job. You may be embarrassed. I too have lost a house to foreclosure. I rebounded.

If you choose to read what someone has to say about how to recover from losing your house; you might learn a thing or two from listening to someone who has actually been through it. I have!

8) Failing To Realize You Must Invest Or You'll Be Doomed To Work For A Living The Rest of Your Life.

You work to gain experience, and learn what you're good at, and what is of value to others. From this work, you may have the opportunity to save, IF YOU DO NOT LIVE BEYOND YOUR MEANS! Soon, you will have some capital thru saving.

You have savings so you can be on the look out for what you can profitably invest in. It is the investing that will free up your time so that you can make better quality decisions, look for new opporutnities and better manage your investments.

The secret to wealth is LEVERAGE. Leverage and capital go together like peanut butter and jelly.

Like I mentioned earlier, RICH PEOPLE, DO WHAT RICH PEOPLE DO. RICH PEOPLE, THINK LIKE RICH PEOPLE.

POOR PEOPLE, THINK LIKE POOR PEOPLE. POOR PEOPLE, DO WHAT POOR PEOPLE DO.

If you choose how to think, and what to think, you will see differences and entirely different results.

Let me give you an example about thinking. I was telling a friend of mine about how exhausting it is and yet frustrating when I'm trying to help someone and they won't listen, or take action. This is very very heurtful to me personally because I know the life that we can all have.

I feel that we should strive to do more to help, and strive for a higher qaulity fo life. My friend told me that I was going about things inefficiently. He told me to stop telling, start writing, and if people what to hear what I have to say, they will pick it up.

What a marvelously simple suggestion! Why hadn't I seen this before? I'll just take my thirty plus years of experiences and all that we've learned and put it into book format. I have made self printed books before and printed them out at Kinkos® (now Fedex Office®) and then gave them out to clients. They were very well received and appreciated by my cleints over the years.

After speaking with one of my friends about expanding the book product offerings, I realized just how his way of thinking was more inclined to help more people.

This book was written to help people, who like me, have lost a home in the past. Although everyone's circumstances are different, the loss was always the same, usually very hurtful.

Somehow, I had failed to pay attention. I had either taken my eyes off my goals, or trusted others to do things they were not qualified to do, or they were simply incompetent, yet I had somehow failed to notice before. Trust me, losing sh!t will make you start paying attention. I think I've made a few key points here and we can agree to move on and rebuild.

In the next and final chapter 12, I go really in depth into the rebuilding process of your financial foundation. In Chapter 12, we focus on case studies specifically and the amounts of money that are recoverable. These are from actual **LOANSMART®** case files we have signed and actually have recovered, or in the process of recovering.

We'll also discuss possible options for using the funds and leveraging the funds recovered to acquire, or control a more valuable asset (aka build wealth).

Here are two forms that are used as evidence in the mortgage recovery equity surplus funds. The first form is a IRS 1099C Cancellation of Debt.

This is the document that IRS REQUIRES that a mortgage company send to both the IRS and the borrower who was foreclosed on. The document is an official federal government document and is used as evidence in court to file for either a civil suit, or a petition for the court to authorize any held funds to the rightful owner.

I mentioned this before, but even thought he funds are there, and available; PROOF MUST BE PROVIDED in order for a claim to be successful.

Following is a copy of a blank 1099C form. The box marked 'Debtor's Name' is the borrower who would be entitled to the mortgage equity surplus funds. Box #1, is the date when the foreclosure event happened. Box #2 is the amount of the debt that was discharged. Box #7 is the amount of the fair market value, or the sale amount of the property.

The amount due to the former owner of the property, aka borrower, is the difference of Box #7 minus Box #2.

Next, we'll turn to where the money is actually located. If the property is located in Maryland, for example, then the funds would be either located in the State of Maryland's Unclaimed Funds Department.

If they are located in the state unclaimed funds, then the form from this state (or your state the property was located in) should be used.

A sample of the Maryland Unclaimed Funds Form is shown following this paragraph here.

COMPTROLLER
of MARYLAND
Serving the People

Control/Claim Number

Unclaimed Property Claim Form & Checklist
Comptroller of Maryland
Compliance Division
Unclaimed Property Unit, 301 West Preston Street
Room 310
Baltimore, Maryland 21201-2385
410-767-1700, or 1-800-782-7383

See attachment for instructions
Please be sure to attach copies of all necessary documentation.

Part A - Claimant Information - Please print clearly

Name of Claimant(s)   Social Security or FEIN Number   Daytime telephone number

Address of Claimant(s)

City, state, zip code

Relationship to original owner   Email Address

Part B - Information on Property claimed - OFFICE USE ONLY

Original owner name   Social Security or FEIN Number

Type of property   Holder name   Amount of Property

Part C - Provide the following documents

☐ Copy of your driver's license or other ID (Required)

☐ Copy of Social Security Card or other documentation containing social security number (Required)

☐ Bank documents (e.g. passbook, bank statement, cancelled check)

☐ Proof of affiliation with:

☐ Letters of Administration   ☐ Small Estate Papers   ☐ True Test Copy of Court Order

☐ Copy of Death Certificate(s) for:

☐ Other:

Part D - Affidavit

Under penalties of perjury, I (we) hereby certify that the foregoing information is true and correct. I (we) further certify that I (we) have not received any property claimed, are entitled to it and know of no other person who claims to be entitled to any portion. I (we) agree to indemnify the state of Maryland and its officers and employees for any loss of claim whatsoever resulting from the payment of this claim to me (us).

X _____
Signature of claimant   Signature of co-claimant

All services provided by the state Comptroller's Office are free. Maryland law provides that you do not have to pay a fee to anyone for assisting you in recovering any property within 24 months of the date it was turned over to this office. Contracts which provide for a fee for such claims are unenforceable.

Part E - For office use only

Claim No.: _____   Control No.: _____   Holder No.: _____

Report Year: _____   Received: _____   Total: $ _____

COT/87 912 Rev. 2/13

Assuming the original lender has foreclosed, discharged the original debt, sold the property at an amount greater then the amount owed, and then turned the property over to the state, or over to the court, following a court ordered foreclosure sale; the funds could be petitioned for recovery via a hearing.

Chapter 12

OPTIONS FOR USING YOUR RECOVERED MORTGAGE EQUITY FUNDS

In the previous chapters, we discussed various strategies for reconnecting the rightful owner with their mortgage surplus equity funds. Assuming the funds are recovered and now in your possession, we'll now look at some case files, the amounts recovered, and what I would do if the money recovered was mine.

Do you remember me discussing earlier, how rich people THINK differently than poor people. Well, considering you may have just come thru a catastrophic financial event; YET NOW HAVE CAPITAL to rebuild your life; I would suggest taking a look at what key successful people have done to LEVERAGE their capital.

Although you may have lost your last house, that shouldn't prevent you from taking a look at acquiring another real estate asset.

While you most likely purchased your last property at the retail level; using a realtor, seeking traditional or even government sponsored financing; I would suggest taking another approach. Rather that purchasing a property on a retail basis, why not consider purchasing wholesale instead?

We'll take a look at **LOANSMART® Case #0599966686**, which involves $390,461.89 mortgage foreclosure surplus equity. This amount is more than enough money to purchase another house, not as a consumer or borrower, but as an investor (being the bank).

So to be clear, this former homeowner, who LOST EVERYTHING, **now has $390,461.89 in potential capital to invest**, and if successful, leverage up to even more.

If it was me and my capital; I'd say to myself "...it's time to start thinking like rich people, and do what they do". Let's look at some potential opportunities to PUT THAT CAPITAL TO WORK.

Opportunity #1 – Tax Lien Certificates & Tax Deed Sales

Buying wholesale with this capital, requires the resolve to go back to the very courts, tax agencies, or lenders that may have foreclosed on you (with capital now in hand) and seeking properties that may have been lost by other borrowers such as yourself.

Some people may think this is unethical, or even illegal. It is NOT! As discussed perviously in this book and in other books in my financial literacy series, the mortgage payment (with impounds) is composed of P.I.T.I which stands for Mortgage Principal, Interest, Taxes and Insurance computed for the yearly cost and divided by 12 equal payments.

If the borrower doesn't make the payments, then the taxes don't get paid, as well as other important bills that come due which are attached to the property. The town, county or city that the property is located in has police, fire departments, schools and a host of other vital and necessary services that the resident need and benefit from.

The teachers, firemen, policemen, etc., MUST BE PAID. In every state, and the District of Columbia, there is a provision of law, which allows the Dept of Revenue Tax Collector to SEIZE any property (including real estate), and then SELL THE PROPERTY AT AUCTION TO PAY THE TAXES! (I'll provide an example here shortly to follow).

This is completely legal. There are two types of tax sales. There is a <u>tax lien sale</u>, and a <u>tax deed sale</u>. With a tax lien sale, when the property taxes are not paid; the tax authority SELLS A CERTIFICATE basically guaranteeing that the purchaser of the certificate will RECIEVE INTEREST at a fixed and predetermined rate, backed by the real estate the property was billed for, but the borrower failed to pay.

With a tax deed sale, which can be at auction, or 'over the counter'; you get ownership of the property. During a tax deed sale auction, you usually bid, and the highest bidder is awarded the property (subject to approval by a judge, or the tax collector or other authorized party); upon immediate payment of a certified funds deposit, and the balance due upon approval.

At some tax deed sale auctions, you may be required to PAY IN FULL via certified funds (cash, cashiers checks, money orders or wire transfers), and you can possibly get the property that day.Just remember this opportunity this way: 1) **Tax Liens Sales** - *you get a piece of paper* (no real estate, YET); 2) **Tax Deeds Sales** – *you get the property*, usually pay way of a special warranty deed, signed off by the Treasurer, the Court or a duly authorized agent.

Like I mentioned, the teachers, firemen, policemen, etc must be paid. So when the borrowers do not pay, the private investors, financial institutions, and other entities can step up to the plate and fill in the gap by buying the IOU's from the county or city treasurers. The collection of tax revenue is a top priority for the treasurers' offices.

If the borrower does not pay, and the taxes aren't collected, the treasurer is authorized by state law to seize the property and sell the real estate at a public auction, usually at the court house steps, or online from a room inside the court house or other designated authorized auction service providers.

States such as Florida pay a maximum of 18% and the bidding (what investors offer to pay goes down from there). Iowa pays 24% for tax lien certificate investors. As mentioned, the treasurers are very serious about collecting the revenues to keep the local governments running.

The treasurer has the power and authority to wipe clean any mortgages or liens from the property and award the property to the tax lien purchasers (after a predetermined amount of time and certain conditions have been met); or alternatively, immediately during a tax deed sale or an 'over the counter' tax sale.

Using my own hometown, Jersey City, NJ, and looking at my own family's tax bill on one property, you can see that there was a <u>tax bill due in the amount of $2,930.52</u> by December 11, 2018 via a tax lien certificate with a maximum interest of 18% per NJ state law R.S. 54:5-1 to R.S. 5-120 and R.S. 40:14A-21 and Chapter 99, P.L. 1997.

This means that if the amount of $2,930.32 isn't paid to the "City of Jersey City Tax Collector" via a cashier's check by close of business December 11, 2018; this property worth over $497,000 will now have a tax lien on the property held by an investor.

The tax lien certificate is capable of earning the investor up to a maximum of 18% interest. Should any property not be redeemed after the tax lien certificate sale; after a certain amount of time passes; it can then go to a tax deed sale, where the mortgages and all other liens are wiped clear of the property.

At an annual rate of return of up to 18%, and ultimately, if the taxes are not paid and the property redeemed; the investor could end up with a special warranty deed from the Tax Deed Sale owning the property "FREE AND CLEAR" worth over $497,000!

That's a whopping potential return of over 16,959% on <u>just one</u> of our family's properties!

A screenshot of the tax sale listing is provided here for educational purposes following along with the full tax sale listing.

For reference, here is an example listing of the tax lien certificate properties (circa 2018).

https://cdnsm5-hosted.civiclive.com/userfiles/servers/server_6189660/file/city%20hall/tax%20collections/jc%20tax%20nov%202018.pdf

<u>Opportunity #1 Summary:</u>

Be Your Own Banker & Invest In Real Estate On The Wholesale, Not Retail Level!

Block	Lot	Qualifier	Owner_Name	Prop_Location	Total_Due
19501	4		FUENTES, ALMA & HOFFMAN, DAVID	87 ATLANTIC ST.	$2,930.52
19501	12		VESPREY, FLOYD	71 ATLANTIC ST.	$169.15
19501	15		BRAVER, MYER	65.5 ATLANTIC STREET	$495.01
19501	17		SKUPIEN, ALINA & ORTIZ, JEROME	63 ATLANTIC ST.	$4,362.96
19501	28		HUDSON VENTURES, LLC	479 M.L. KING DRIVE	$2,843.74
19501	32		RAMOS,RICARDO	144 UNION ST.	$4,144.47
19501	34		MAHABIR LARRY SOOKDEO	146.5 UNION STREET	$304.75
19501	38		BANKS, NORMA	152 UNION ST.	$1,752.33
19501	45		SOUL SAVING CHURCH OF GOD IN CHRIST	166 UNION ST.	$675.76

City of Jersey City

TAX SALE NOTICE

FOR UNPAID REAL ESTATE TAXES, WATER/SEWER CHARGES, AND/OR OTHER MUNICIPAL CHARGES:

PUBLIC NOTICE IS HEREBY GIVEN THAT I, ANTHONY ESPOSITO, ACTING TAX COLLECTOR OF TAXES, FOR THE CITY OF JERSEY CITY, COUNTY OF HUDSON, STATE OF NEW JERSEY, WILL SELL AT PUBLIC AUCTION, AT CITY HALL, 280 GROVE STREET, JERSEY CITY, NEW JERSEY ON:

THURSDAY DECEMBER 13, 2018 AT 9:00 A.M.
THE FOLLOWING DESCRIBED DELINQUENT CHARGES.

THE AMOUNT SET FOURTH BELOW REPRESENTS A STATEMENT OF CURRENT OR PRIOR TAXES, WATER/ SEWER AND OTHER MUNICIPAL CHARGES AGAINST THE PROPERTY EXISTING ON NOVEMBER 11, 2018 TOGETHER WITH **INTEREST AND COSTS ON ALL ITEMS COMPUTED TO DECEMBER 13, 2018.** THE SALE WILL BE CONDUCTED IN ACCORDANCE WITH THE PROVISIONS OF THE NEW JERSEY STATUES R.S. 54:5-1 TO R.S. 54:5-120 AND R.S. 40:14A-21 AND CHAPTER 99, P.L.1997, AND THE ACTS AMENDATORY THEREOF AND THERETO THE SUBSCRIBER WILL SELL IN FEE TO THE PERSON WHO BIDS THE AMOUNT DUE, SUBJECT TO REDEMPTION AT THE LOWEST RATE OF INTEREST BUT IN NO CASE EXCEEDING 18 (EIGHTEEN) PER CENT.

IMPORTANT PLEASE NOTE:
IN ORDER FOR YOU TO REMOVE YOUR PROPERTY FROM THIS TAX SALE YOU MUST:
(A) DRAW A CERTIFIED CHECK TO THE "CITY OF JERSEY CITY TAX COLLECTOR" FOR THE AMOUNT INDICATED BELOW.
(B) PERSONAL CHECKS, BUSINESS CHECKS, CREDIT UNION CHECKS WILL NOT BE ACCEPTED. PAYMENTS MUST BE IN CASH, CERTIFIED CHECK OR A MONEY ORDER ONLY.
(C)ALL PAYMENTS MUST BE RECEIVED BY THE CLOSE OF THE BUSINESS DAY ON TUESDAY DECEMBER 11, 2018.
(D) HOMEOWNERS IN THE US MILITARY ON ACTIVE DUTY MAY CONTACT THE
TAX COLLECTOR AT(201)547-5526 TO COMPLETE FORM AMSPTD

INDIVIDUALS PURCHASING LIENS
(A) MUST REQUEST A VENDOR NUMBER BY WEDNESDAY 3:00 PM DECEMBER 12, 2018 IN THE TAX COLLECTOR'S OFFICE *$1,000.00 DOWN PAYMENT IS REQUIRED FOR FIRST TIME BIDDERS. *CERTIFIED CHECKS/ MONEY ORDERS WILL ONLY BE ACCEPTED FOR THE $1000.00 DOWN PAYMENT. BIDDER NUMBERS WILL BE GIVEN OUT ON THURSDAY 12-13-18
(B) PAYMENTS FOR ITEMS PURCHASED WILL BE ACCEPTED IN CERTIFIED CHECKS, MONEY ORDERS, OR A WIRE TRANSFER, ALL PAYMENTS MUST BE MADE BY THE CLOSE OF THE BUSINESS DAY OR THE ITEM WILL BE PUT BACK INTO THE TAX SALE.
© PLEASE BE ADVISED THAT THE PROPERTIES LISTED BELOW MAY BE SUBJECT TO THE "ENVIRON-

By the way, we paid the taxes.

Now, as a potential investor, would I utilize the capital of $2,930.52 and re-invest to make 18% or even possibly as high as 16,959%? ABSOLUTELY! You bet I would! That's why I've chosen to place this opportunity as one of the top options to leverage wealth and get you back to where you should have been if you didn't lose your property before.

The loss happened. It's a temporary set-back, at best!

Opportunity #2 – Cognition & Miscognition

When asked on how to make investment decisions to enjoy prosperity and longevity during an interview, Mr. Charles Munger, the Vice Chair of Berkshire Hathaway stated facts about the standard human condition. Most interestingly Mr. Munger named 'Cognition' and 'MisCognition' as one of the primary factors affecting the condition of wealth & poverty. (YouTube: "Charlie Munger's Advice on Investing & Life Choices – Yahoo Finance").

Simply put, paraphrasing, the standard human condition is ignorance and stupidity! You can take advantage of other people by "….eliminating you own miscognition.". To understand what Mr. Munger is saying, perhaps we should re-visit the dictionary definition of "miscognition", and "cognition", just to make sure we're clearly receiving his advice. So here is what my Google search reveals from the Oxford Language definition along with my summary of what I found for it's opposite:

cog-ni-tion

noun: cognition

the mental action or process of <u>acquiring</u> knowledge and understanding through thought, experience, and the <u>senses</u>. Also know as 'thinking'.

> ### miscognition
>
> *noun: miscognition*
>
> the opposite of cognition. Also, incorrect or false 'thinking'. A sense of being unprepared; a wrong way of thinking.

Mr. Charlie Munger has spent nearly his entire life trying to avoid making stupid mistakes. So when it comes to recovering from mistakes, as I've made, and perhaps you've made; **Charlie Munger** is certainly someone we should consider what he has to say in this book about mortgage foreclosure recovery.

I encourage you to listen to **Mr. Munger's** interview for your own deductions. Simply put, **Mr. Munger** is saying that we make mistakes because of our flawed way of thinking and to ensure our own success; **we should eliminate our own miscognitions, or our own stupid thinking.**

I could simply insert a cliché and say "....invest in yourself. Or educate yourself.". But that wouldn't necessarily produce a favorable and sustainable change aka progress. Just because you read a book, or educate yourself, doesn't mean you won't repeat the very same mistakes and subscribe to the 'flawed thinking' that led one of our property taxes to become delinquent and a $497,000 asset to be at risk. In my own family's case, like most people, the mortgage payment includes the principal, interest, taxes and insurance (PITI), if there are impounds in the mortgage contract.

If there are no impounds, then the property owners are responsible for paying the taxes, and the insurance as it comes due. Alarmingly, even if you have a mortgage payment with impounds, YOUR ANNUAL PROPERTY TAX PAYMENTS MIGHT NOT BE MADE BY THE MORTGAGE COMPANY ON TIME! In this case, the property would then have to be redeemed by either the mortgage company or the property owner paying the tax lien certificate with interest.

In the context of this last Chapter 12 in this book, the **"LOANSMART® MORTGAGE FORECLOSURE RECOVERY GUIDE - *A Definitive Guide For Anyone Who's Lost Their Home To Foreclosure!"*,** I'm focusing briefly on a few important things in the recovery process that should be considered. I'm not covering ALL the things that should be considered, just some of them.

To be clear, THERE CAN BE NO SUSTAINING RECOVERY WITHOUT CHANING YOUR WAY OF THINKING!

You absolutely will have to change your way of thinking. If you don't, any progress, or changes you implement or commit to, could lead you right back to losses. <u>Every mistake you make</u>, is **AN OPPORTUNITY FOR YOU TO LEARN!**

Every negative, expressed as a symbol or **<u>A LINE</u>** as seen below, is nothing but a **potential positive, waiting for you to put your line thru it!**

━━━━━━━

For example, you may have experienced a foreclosure, lost a property due to tax forfeiture, or any number of reasons I listed in part in the "Introduction" of this book. Though painful, YOU LEARNED WHAT CAN HAPPENED! You've been thru it. Now, you are aware of the existence of the opportunity to buy properties, or even invest in them passively, without doing any work, and making more interest safely that you would if you left your mortgage equity surplus funds in the bank.

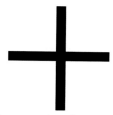

Because of what you've learned, you can put your capital to work and passively make 5%, 18%, 24% or even 36% on the tax lien certificates.

If you take action, and apply what you've learned, then the negative line or mark, now gets a line thru it! **The negative is NOW A PLUS OR <u>POSITIVE</u> MARKER IN YOUR LIFE.** If you get negative marks, look for ways to convert them to a positive, rather than dwell on the temporary state of what happened being negative. These events, such as foreclosure, are only permanent IF YOU LET THEM BE PERMANENT!

I used **Charlie Munger** as an example. There are many examples of people who have common sense, and THINK. No matter what your religion, race, creed, or color, there are like minded people who are willing to share their thoughts, of which, you may meditate, and draw from these insights. So what I've been suggesting from opportunities #1, and 2 is to 1) Put your capital to work for you; and 2) Change your thinking to align with those who are successful. If you find that you're surrounded by negative thinking people, look to YouTube or Google topics of your interest. You should quickly find people to "sit in" on their conversations. All it takes is just one idea during their published-shared conversations to ignite a thought in your mind, and lead you down a whole new way of thinking which could lead to a new life of successes in your life. Here are a few of my favorites to get you started below.

Earn Your Leisure (EYL)™

Most recently, I've become fascinated with the Entrepreneurial Leadership of "**Earn Your Leisure™ aka EYL™**" founded in 2019 by **Troy Millings**, **Rashad Bilal** and **Ian Dunlap**.

Earn Your Leisure™ is a college business class, mixed with pop culture powered by a self-created & owned media platform with millions of followers across multiple social media platforms.

They share my priority, Financial Literacy, and I'm also a firm believer in their motto "Assets Over Liabilities", now a multi-category brand. I'm searching their website for my sizes in their merch right now (4XL by the way). They place a particular emphasis on people of color, such as myself, who historically lack access to financial tools and resources; it's only right that I mention them first. Be sure to check out their podcast:

https://www.iheart.com/podcast/256-earn-your-leisure-31087183/

and their website at:

https://www.earnyourleisure.com .

I also found the Black Enterprise® article on them very insightful.

Check out: https://www.blackenterprise.com/how-earn-your-leisure-is-transforming-financial-literacy-for-the-culture/

There is a lot of high quality content produced regularly by the **EYL Network™** that can help you learn and stay motivated as you rebuild your financial life available for you. You can join EYL University™ for a modest investment of $97/month and I would argue successfully that this is the **best educational value** anywhere on the planet for the cost:

https://www.eyluniversity.com/joinnow?

(Good Faith Disclosure - No commissions earned from this referral)

Social Proof

For those of you who dream about leaving your day job, and transitioning to your dream job, I have just the Man for you. Meet **Mr. David Shands**, a former waiter, who one day woke up and realized he was going to start right where he was working at Cheesecake Factory®, and create his own platform to tirelessly help others succeed.

Mr. Shands is a serial entrepreneur who founded **"The Social Proof Podcast™"**, **"Sleep is For Suckers™"**, and **"The Morning Meetup™"** at:

https://www.thesocialproofpodcast.com

https://sleepisforsuckers.com

https://www.themorningmeetup.com

As featured in **Forbes®** Magazine, **David Shands** said "…..there is potential of the podcast industry as IP. I'm able to cross promote and the IP can be used everywhere!". You can check out the Forbes article below:

https://www.forbes.com/sites/joshwilson/2022/07/06/ podcasts-are-increasingly-being-adapted-for-television/? sh=203764b22a9e

Mr. Shands "The Morning Meet Up" is a great value for only $79/month giving you access to hundreds of like minded business & success experts with REAL WORLD experiences. Visit it here:

https://www.themorningmeetup.com/

(Good Faith Disclosure - No commissions earned from this referral)

Charlie Chang & His $128,000/mo Income

If you're still wondering about the options for our client and what he should do with his capital of $390,461.89, it would be a huge mistake to overlook **Charlie Chang**. **Mr. Chang** practices a multi-stream income approach, otherwise known as 'income diversification".

Mr. Chang is also a serial entrepreneur like the previous entrepreneurs, who is an investor and who owns multiple businesses. I really don't want to spoil the surprise for you about Charlie, and I really can't tell his story as good as he can. I'll let him explain his amazing monthly income stream, and how he does it from his video below:

https://www.youtube.com/watch?v=uhUeROuQN-8

(Good Faith Disclosure - No commissions earned from this referral)

Humbled Trader

With over 1,000,000+ subscribers across multiple social media platforms, the "**Humbled Trader**" is **Sharon Huang, aka Shay**! To quote her, "…..Are you tired of all the Lambos, the luxury travel and partying you see in day trading ads? I am too! And I promise you won't see any of that here…" on her channel.

Shay, aka the "Humbled Trader" has a whopping 47,000,000+ views on her YouTube channel alone where she teaches people how to daytrade. In one video, I watched her literally make over $15,000 in just one day!

I'm very found of her and her style because there is no fluff, long winded talk filled with pipe dreams and wishes. As she states about her channel, "….(My) This is a channel made by a day trader, for day traders who are REAL. Stock market trading and investing is hard. Seeing all the fluff out there on social media creates unrealistic expectations for beginners new to day trading. ". You gotta love her. If you'd like to subscribe to her channel and learn more about how she makes money, it won't cost you much for all the information you can get. Here's her link below:

https://community.humbledtrader.com/a/43426/e7ZzsnBk

(Good Faith Disclosure: I earn a small commission from her link thru this book)

My younger clients would consider me a dinosaur, out of touch, and devoid of all credibility if I didn't mention in this book the hottest technology that technically savvy are using to make money and that is **ChatGPT** by **OpenAI**.

I know about **AI** because for the last 5+ years, I've been experimenting and building an **AI** platform in the **FinTech** space where the mortgage industry and customers are most likely to meet, converge & have a pleasant experience.   In short, it takes a lot of time to **TRAIN AI** to be responsive, factual, credible, and to give the appropriate desired outcome. I've had a hunch that a lot of people are going to forgo using their laptops, computers, and tablets to complete a mortgage loan application. I think they will simply ASK their ambient computing enabled device to help them get a loan. I've been working on this, and progress is being made. Just try asking Amazon's Alexa® about certain mortgage related questions and you'll hear the **LOANSMART®** brand at work. But progress is not just limited in one area.

That's why when **Shay,** the "**Humbled Trader**" shows us how she uses **ChatGPT AI** to make her a $100,000 trading strategy _WITH ZERO CODING KNOWLEDGE_, I was intrigued! There's a lot to learn. But for those willing to learn, people like our client with the $390,461.89 in capital might want to invest some time and a few bucks to see if growth is possible.

Opportunity #2 Summary:

Change Your Way of Thinking! Learn How Successful People Think. Consider Doing What Successful People Do. It Will Fast Track Your Financial Recovery And Save Years of Wasted Time In Reaching Your New Goals.

Opportunity #3 – Financial Leverage

Financial leverage is necessary to maximize your advantages to achieve your goal. So what is the goal to be achieved with financial leverage you may ask?

Financial leverage is the art of using capital, credit or another resource to purchase, or control another asset of greater or appreciating value. The 'spread' is the difference between the 'cost' of the capital or other resource, and the value of the asset, otherwise known as PROFIT.

There are many ways to use financial leverage; and this leverage does not always have to be money. It can be your money. It can be other people's money (I.E. Credit) or it can be a trade of your time, connections or other assets and resources.

While we are on the subject of money.

"In my opinion, there is a difference between the word 'money' and the word 'capital'. Money is something you tender in exchange for goods and services. Capital is something that is invested with the timely expectation of a profitable return."

We started this chapter by considering *what I would do* with the client's $390,461.89 in recovered mortgage foreclosure equity surplus which is now CAPITAL, and not money. If it is deployed, **it must provide a profitable return.**

While there are many options to consider in deploying this capital, we've touched on a few, but certainly not all. You may have considered:

- Starting a business
- Buying a business
- Investing in the stock market or options trading
- Forex Trading
- Going to college to get or complete a degree
- Lending money to family, friends or colleagues
- Writing a book & publishing it
- Taking a vacation

- Investing in Intellectual Property
- Donating to charity or another worthwhile cause

Any of the aforementioned activities would be a good reward or a good return if it lifts your spirits and makes you feel better about yourself. Granted, but that's not why I wrote this book. I wrote this book to help you consider how to recover from a mortgage foreclosure by showing you the benefit of conducting a mortgagor servicing audit to determine (and prove) if the payments made were properly recorded, if there was equity in the property when it was lost, and if so, how to go about recovering the funds so you can begin the process of rebuilding your life.

It is a common misconception that if you've lost your home to foreclosure, that you've lost everything, and you're no longer entitled to the mortgage foreclosure equity surplus funds. This is not correct.

In previous chapters, I've convered basic principals about recovering your mortgage funds. Assuming you've recovered the funds now, and you've learned from your mistakes; **you must make it your TOP PRIORITY to analyze opportunities to use the funds you now have to control an INCOME PRODUCING ASSET (or assets) that is worth more than the funds you have recovered.** Many people have dreamed of starting a business and owning a business. From experience, I can tell you that you will feel a great sense of pride when you 'arrive at a business' that you've built from scratch. It's a dream that becomes a reality for many people.

However, it is also a dream that millions of people fail to achieve. If given the choice, based on my experience; I WOULD THINK HARD AND LONG ABOUT STARTING A BUSINESS VERSUS BUYING AN ALREADY SUCCESSFUL BUSINESS!

WHY?

There is a steep learning curve to go from starting a new business and figuring out what works; to actually becoming successful and profitable. While you travel through the learning curve; you'll be BURNING THE INVESTOR'S CASH (MEANING YOURS)!

Conversely, if you decide to PURCHASE AN EXISTING BUSINESS THAT IS ALREADY PROFITABLE & SUCCESSFUL, before you spend a single dime of your capital; you can look and learn, how the business operates, ways to improve profitability, and be profitable from day one of ownership with the right due diliigence. There is no

145

shortgage of successful business people willing to 'sell their baby', their successful and profitable business; to someone who will really 'give it their all' and keep the former owner's business going.

I know this because I speak with these owners nearly everyday. Some are saddened that they are unable to pass their businesses on to their children or family members. In some instances, these are people who have built multi-million dollar businesses out of nothing but sensing opportunity, seizing it, and hard work (or should I say 'smart' work). Yet, their children have NO INTEREST IN CONTINUING THEIR SUCCESSFUL LEGACY!

This is an excellent opportunity for you! Now that you have CAPITAL; you have more resources to get back on your feet. If you've lost your home, you've been kicked in the gut, so to speak and suffered a deep loss. Yet, you've have survived! Hopefully this book will help give you some ideas and encourage you to take action.

"Start where you're at!
Use what you've got!
Finish what you start!"
- David E. Hoffman Jr.

Opportunity #3 Summary

Use your capital to acquire something that's more valuable that your investment and makes you income!

A) You can start a business, or better yet, use some of your capital to purchase an already profitable business with a proven track record from a retiring owner. It is a much faster path to success if you purchase a business that has the revenue to pay you the salary you need to live comfortably than to start one from scratch.

B) You can purchase an income producing property with a high occupancy rate and low delinquency rate. Over the years I've had countless foreign investors come to the United States seeking to acquire income producing properties with little or no credit! With my LOANSMART® case files as my resource along with all the datapoints to back me; we introduced these clients to licensed realtors, attorneys and others who helped them close purchase transactions. The income of the property was used to qualify the buyers. There's no reason that you shouldn't be able to do this also.

C) Consider starting a blog, or YouTube channel to share your story of what you've been through in your foreclosure experience. Although the experience may have been painful,

I've found interesting ways to help people HEAL from their loss by talking about it. I often pay past foreclosure homeowners to come to new homebuyers seminars where I speak to provide REAL LIFE knowledge to the prospective home buyers. They leave the seminars with a HEIGHTENED SENSIVITY to foreclosure and what not to do. It's very insightful when I ask former homeowners to share with the group "...what they've learned and what they would do the next time".

If you've lost your home, your blog where you tell your story becomes "digital real estate", and your blog articles are the content that will drive readers to your pages. Once readers are at your blog, you can offer advertisers and affiliate partners a place for their ads or promotions (for a fee of course). This new sideline income can grow very quickly and exponentially if you're a good writer, post frequently, and use keywords that are likely to attract readers. I know a few bloggers who have left their former full time jobs and make over $20,000 each month from their blogs, advertising and affiliate promotions. The advertising is a source of income just for you placing the ads on your blog pages. **Everytime you create a blog post, you're creating digital real estate, which you can in turn sell more ads.**

Affiliate promotions usually don't pay for ads, but they pay nice commissions if the visits from your pages convert into actual sales.

I remember the very first time I made my first commision from an affiliate link. I had a LOANSMART® blog that was published on Amazon's Kindle Blogs. At the time, Amazon was allowing blog owners to publish blogs on their platform. I intially charged .99/cents for my LOANSMART® digital product, the blog, and my content as then and now, focuses on the mortgage bank services industry. I wrote content of interest to homeowners, prospective homeowners, client who I already closed mortgage loans for, and I even setup triggers that would allow them to download their LOANSMART® Equity Management Report to their mobile devices.

Of course, I had sold advertising spaces on all the pages which surrounded my creative content , based on my LOANSMART® Case files. To my total amazement, I got any email notice out of the blue after my blog launch of a $157 payout! An affiliate promotion I has placed for Comcast (back then but now xFinity) had paid me commissions because several people who had read my blog posts, also decided they would take advantage of the Comcast offer I shared with visitors on my blog. I had done absolutelu nothing but paste the few lines of code on the blog which automatically displayed the tiny little ads. Comcast wasn't the only business I entered into this type of business transaction with. I also placed ads for Lynda.com (my favorite) and back then, they paid really well. I also placed ads for real estate brokerages too! It goes without saying the some advertisers pay really well for Cost Per Mil (CPM) advertising.

So don't overlook the opportunity to simply create a blog, start sharing your story about any experience you desire, creating digital real estate and then earning income from the ads you placed on your newly created digital real estate.

The things I've shared in this book are for educational and informational purposes only. They are not intented to be investment, financial or legal advice.

It's always advisable to seek the advice of professionals who can further assist you in achieving your goals. I have a practical rule about advice that I adopted from a billionaire friend of mine long ago. He told me, "...Dave, if you want to learn how to become a billionaire, seek the advice from a billionaire who's done it. If you want to learn how to become the successful owner of a profitable mortgage brokerage, learn from someone who's already done it. In fact, anything you want to do, look for someone who's ALREADY DONE IT!".

His sentiment could be any harsher when I asked him one day, "...hey, there's a conference coming to town next week and I wanted to know if you'd go with me?".

My billionaire friend looked at the promotional printout they sent me and that I just shared with him for all of about 10 seconds. "DEFINITELY NOT INTERESTED!", was his reply.

Confused, I asked, "....but you're the very one who's always encouraged me to learn! So here I am asking you to go to this thing with me so we can learn, and you shoot me down right away like I just asked to sleep with your wife or something! What gives?".

He laughed, and replied "....Dave, the reason I said no so quickly is because you handed me something promotional which WANTS ME TO PAY THEM $1000 BUCKS TO ATTEND A CONFERENCE to supposedly learn from a bunch of gurus about how to get rich? It's a joke. None of my business associates will be there (unless theyre GETTING

PAID TO BE THERE)! Trust me I know a few wealthy people myself.", he said.

After I thought about what my wealthy friend had said, I realized he was right.

If you want to learn how to do anything, learn from someone's who's done it; not from someone who talks about doing it. We laughed it off that day. The lessons remain with me. And from my friend, who shall remain nameless, these words are from him to you:

"In Texas, we have a saying – Big Hat, No Cattle."

I'll leave your interpretation of this saying to your own mind.

Conclusion

In this book, I've taken the time to summarize experiences from many case files of borrowers, applicants & investors I served over the years in my mortgage industry practice. It would be a waste to not share what I've learned particularly if it helps someone get their lives back on track after a traumatic event such as losing a home to foreclosure.

Although this is emotionally and financially devasting; it certainly is not the end of your life's journey nor your family's progress. It is my sincere hope that this book will help someone who has suffered recover. While this book is a product of my years of mortgage experiences and the insights I've gained; IT IS NOT MEANT TO BE FINANCIAL NOR LEGAL ADVICE. This book is for educational and entertainment purposes only specifically geared to those consumers of mortgage products and services. My LOANSMART® brand is used as a way to distinctly identify myself from others also in the mortgage baking & services industry.

The LOANSMART® brand is an indicator of the origin or source of products and services that allows you to spend less time on research when seeking credible information in the mortgage industry marketplace.

I have earned a reputaion from real world experience, case by case, challenge by challenge since my journey in the industry began over 30+ years ago. I've helped many people faces obstacles, overcome challenges to homeownership and even recover successfully after losing everything.

I could not have done this without the help of very talented professionals at title & escrow companies, law offices, real estate brokerages, insurance companies, and even judges! I AM HONORED TO BE TRUSTED WITH THEIR BUSINESS and work with them all. Any feedback or testimonies you hear or find is the emoitional connection that they share with the LOANSMART® brand AS A RESULT OF THE RESULTS we've attained for them.

Thank You and Good Luck on Your Journey!

###

DISCLAIMER: I strongly suggest that you seek the advice of COMPETENT LEGAL COUNSEL, and make a list of any questions that came to mind as a result of reading this book. Then, armed with your questions, you are better positioned to have a knowledgeable and intelligent conversation with the Attorney, CPA or Certified Financial Advisor of your own choosing. Not every advisor is competent, so due your due diligence on them first.